THE STATE

Edited by Viviene E. Cree

First published in Great Britain in 2015 by

Policy Press
University of Bristol
1-9 Old Park Hill
Bristol
BS2 8BB
UK
t: +44 (0)117 954 5940
pp-info@bristol.ac.uk
www.policypress.co.uk

North America office:
Policy Press
c/o The University of Chicago Press
1427 East 60th Street
Chicago, IL 60637, USA
t: +1 773 702 7700
f: +1 773-702-9756
sales@press.uchicago.edu
www.press.uchicago.edu

ISBN 978-1-4473-2197-2 Paperback
ISBN 978-1-4473-2199-6 ePub
ISBN 978-1-4473-2198-9 Kindle

British Library Cataloguing in Publication Data
A catalogue record for this book is available from the British Library.

Library of Congress Cataloging-in-Publication Data
A catalog record for this book has been requested.

Cover design by Policy Press
Printed in Great Britain by www.4edge.co.uk

ALSO AVAILABLE IN THIS SERIES

Contents

Contributors

Gary Clapton is a Senior Lecturer in Social Work at the University of Edinburgh. He specialises in adoption and fostering, child welfare and protection and fathers. His work includes *Social work with fathers: Positive practice* (2013) and a number of papers directed to changing current policies and practices in Scotland.

Viviene E. Cree is Professor of Social Work Studies at the University of Edinburgh. She is a qualified youth and community and social worker. She has carried out extensive research into social work history, the profession and children's services and has published widely. A recent book is *Becoming a social worker: Global narratives* (2013).

William Fear is a chartered psychologist with a specialist interest in discourse analysis in organisational settings. He trained at Cardiff University School of Psychology and is particularly interested in the role of narrative in the construction of institutions and the use of language-based artefacts such as texts and stories.

Jim Greer is Principal Lecturer in Social Work at Teesside University. He is a registered social worker, a project manager and a member of the British Psychological Society. His interests are mental health, management and service improvement, use of new technologies in social care, and free speech and personal liberty.

Neil Hume is a social worker in a local authority children and families' team in the North-East of Scotland. Previously he worked for several years in various criminal justice settings in Edinburgh.

Steve Kirkwood is a Lecturer in Social Work at the University of Edinburgh, with a focus on criminal justice, asylum seekers and research methods. His research involves a range of topics broadly related to justice and identity; he is originally from Wellington, New

Zealand. A recent publication, *Researching celebrity historic sexual abuse allegations* (2014), is jointly authored with Mark Smith, Clare Llewellyn and Ros Burnett.

Elias Le Grand teaches social theory at the Department of Sociology, Stockholm University. A cultural sociologist, his research interests are in consumer culture, identity formation, socio-spatial divisions and youths. A recent publication is 'Class, community and belonging in a "chav town", in *Mobilities and neighbourhood belonging in cities and suburbs* (2014), edited by Paul Watt and Peer Smets.

David McKendrick is a Lecturer in Social Work at Glasgow Caledonian University. He is interested in fear and its impact on social work practice.

Mark Smith is a Senior Lecturer and current Head of Social Work at the University of Edinburgh. He has an interest in abuse allegations made against care staff and is currently working on an ESRC-funded project centred on allegations against the former BBC disc jockey, Jimmy Savile. One of his recent books is *Residential child care in practice: Making a difference* (2013), written with Leon Fulcher and Peter Doran.

Series editors' preface

Viviene E. Cree, Gary Clapton and Mark Smith

This book series begins and ends with a question: how useful are ideas of moral panic to the social issues and anxieties that confront us today? Forty years on from the publication of Stan Cohen's seminal study *Folk Devils and Moral Panics*, does this remain a helpful way of thinking about social concerns, or should the concept be consigned to the sociological history books as an amusing, but ultimately flawed, theoretical device? 'Moral panic' is, after all, one of the foremost sociological terms that has crossed over from academic to public discourse; in doing so, it has lost a great deal of its rigour and, arguably, its value. All the contributors to the series are, in their own ways, engaging critically with the relevance of moral panic ideas for their own understandings of some of the most pressing personal, professional and political concerns of the day. They do not all come up with the same conclusions, but they do agree that moral panics – no matter how we think of them – focus on the social issues that worry us most.

The book series takes forward findings from an Economic and Social Research Council (ESRC) sponsored research seminar series that ran between 2012 and 2014 at events across the UK. The seminar series was designed to mark the 40th anniversary of *Folk Devils and Moral Panics*; and to bring together international and UK academics, researchers and practitioners from a range of disciplines to debate and discuss moral panics in the 21st century. The three main organisers had, independently of one another, written about events and happenings that had caused great anxiety within social work and within society as a whole: satanic abuse (Clapton, 1993); sex trafficking (Cree, 2008); abuse in residential childcare (Smith, 2008 and 2010). In each case, we had challenged accepted accounts of the issues and asked questions about the real-life (often negative) consequences of holding particular conceptualisations of these difficult topics. We had not, at that time, used the concept of moral panic as the foremost tool for analysis, but we had all been interested in the ideas of discourse, labelling, deviancy amplification and social control, all of which connect with ideas of moral panic. With the 40th anniversary imminent, we saw this as offering an opportunity to revisit this, asking: what relevance does the idea of moral panic have for an examination of 21st-century social issues and anxieties?

The seminar series produced a number of outcomes: articles, blogs and the collection of papers included in these bytes. However, the collection is broader than the seminar series in two key ways: firstly, some chapters were especially commissioned because it was felt that there was a gap in the collection or because the writer had a particularly interesting approach to the issues; secondly, each of the books in this series ends with an afterword written by a social work practitioner who has been invited to reflect on the contributions from the perspective of practice. This demonstrates not only our commitment to knowledge exchange more generally, but also our belief that moral panic ideas have special relevance for social work.

Moral panics and social work

Although 'moral panic' is a sociological idea that has widespread intellectual interest, it has, as Cohen (1998) acknowledges, special relevance for social work. Social work as an academic discipline and a profession plays a central role in the process of defining social issues and then trying to do something about them – that is our job! So we have to be particularly alert to the part we play within this. We are, in moral panic parlance, 'moral entrepreneurs' and 'claims makers': we tell society (government, policy makers, other practitioners, members of the public) what the social problems are, how they should be understood and how they should be addressed. We do so, in 21st-century terms, through secular, professional and academic discourse, but at heart, what we are expressing is a set of ideas about how we should live and what it is to be human. In other words, we remain a 'moral' and, at times, moralising profession.

The concept of moral panic reminds us that our deeply held attitudes and values have origins and consequences in the real world, both positive and negative. And sometimes they are not the origins or consequences we expect them to be. Hence the lens of moral panic highlights the ways in which social issues that begin with real concerns may lead to the labelling and stigmatising of certain behaviours and individuals; they may precipitate harsh and disproportionate legislation; they may make people more fearful and society a less safe place. Focusing on some social issues may distract attention away from other, underlying concerns; so a focus on trafficking may, for example, ignore the realities of repressive, racist immigration policies, just as a focus on internet pornography may lead to legislation that undermines individual freedom, and a focus on child protection may inhibit our capacity to support families, as Featherstone et al (2014) have identified. These are not issues about which we, as editors and contributors to this series, have answers – but we do have questions. And it is our firm belief that social work must engage with these questions if we are to practise in ways that are truly emancipatory and in line with the social work profession's social justice principles.

A particular moment in the history of moral panics?

The years 2013 and 2014 have proved to be a very particular time in the history of moral panics for two, very different, reasons. The first reason is that a number of key protagonists from the early theoretical writing on deviance, moral panics and the state died in 2013 and early 2014.

- Stan Cohen, sociologist and author of *Folk Devils and Moral Panics* (1972), *Visions of Social Control* (1985), *States of Denial* (2001) and numerous other publications, died in January 2013.
- Geoffrey Pearson, social work professor and author of *The Deviant Imagination* (1975) and *Hooligan: A History of Respectable Fears* (1983), died in April 2013.

- Jock Young, criminologist and author of *The Drugtakers* (1971) and many other studies including, most recently, *The Criminological Imagination* (2011), died in November 2013.
- Stuart Hall, critical theorist, founding editor of *New Left Review* and author with Charles Critcher and others of *Policing the Crisis* (1978), died in February 2014.

We wished to mark the contribution of these great thinkers, and so we have included a commentary on one of them within each byte in the series. This is not to suggest that they are the only people who have written about contemporary social issues in this way; in fact, Geoffrey Pearson was more concerned with the persistent nature of what he called 'respectable discontents' than about the sporadic eruptions of moral panics. But, as the series will demonstrate, theorists from a wide range of academic disciplines have continued to engage with the concept of moral panics over the 40-plus years since 1972, sometimes arguing for its continuing value (for example, Goode and Ben-Yehuda, 1994) and at other times favouring alternative explanations, such as those around risk (for example, Beck, 1992, 1999) and moral regulation (for example, Hunt, 1999). More recently, scholars have attempted to move 'beyond the heuristic', to develop a way of thinking about moral panic that both informs, and continues 'to be informed by, movements and developments in social theory' (Rohloff and Wright, 2010, p 419).

The second reason why this has been a special time is because of what has been called the 'Jimmy Savile effect' in numerous press and media reports. It is difficult to discuss the scandal around Jimmy Savile, TV presenter and prolific sex offender, who died in October 2011, in a dispassionate way. In September and October 2012, almost a year after his death, claims emerged that Savile had committed sexual abuse over many years, with his victims ranging from girls and boys to adults. By October 2012, allegations had been made to 13 British police forces, and a series of inquiries followed. The revelations around the Jimmy Savile affair encouraged others to come forward and claim that they had been abused by celebrities: Stuart Hall (TV presenter, not critical theorist), Rolf Harris, Max Clifford and many others have been investigated and prosecuted. These events have encouraged us to ask wider questions in articles and blogs about physical and sexual abuse, and about potentially negative fall-out from the furore around historic abuse. This has not been easy: how do we get across the reality that we are not minimising the damage that abuse can cause, while at the same time calling for a more questioning approach to victimisation and social control? These questions remain challenging as we move forward.

The series

This series of bytes introduces a collection of papers that engage with a social issue through the lens of moral panic. It will be evident from the chapters that, as editors, we have not imposed a 'moral panic straightjacket' on the contributors; nor do we hold to the notion that there is one 'Moral Panic Theory' with a capital T. Instead, contributors have been invited to consider moral panic ideas very broadly, focusing on their capacity to add to a deeper understanding of the social problem under discussion. Because of this, the series offers a number of opportunities for those who are already familiar with the concept of moral panic and for those who are not. For those who have been thinking about moral panic ideas for years, the series will serve as a new 'take' on some of the puzzling aspects of moral panic theories. For those who are coming across the notion of moral panic for the first time, or have only everyday knowledge of it, the case-study examples of particular social issues and anxieties contained in each chapter will serve as an introduction not only to moral panic as a theoretical concept, but also to what, we hope, might become a new avenue of critical inquiry for readers in the future.

The series is divided into four short volumes ('bytes'): *Gender and family*; *Childhood and youth*; *The state*; and *Moral regulation*. Each byte contains an introduction, which includes a short retrospective on one of the four early theorists whom we have already identified. Five chapters follow, each exploring the case study of one social issue, asking how useful a moral panic lens is (or is not) to understanding this social problem. Each byte ends with an afterword written by a social work practitioner. The four bytes are also available as a single volume – *Revisiting moral panics*, featuring an introduction to Moral Panic Theory by Charles Critcher – with the aim of reaching as wide an audience as possible.

The books in this series should be read as an opening conversation. We are not seeking either consensus or closure in publishing this series; quite the opposite, our aim is to ask questions – of social problems, of professional practice and of ourselves. In doing so, we pay homage to Cohen's (1998, p 112) challenge to 'stay unfinished'; instead of seeking to resolve the contradictions and complexities that plague theory and practice, we must, he argues, be able to live with ambiguity. The series may help us and others to do just that, and, in doing so, may contribute towards the building of a more tolerant, open social work practice and a more tolerant, open society.

Acknowledgement

With thanks to the ESRC for funding the seminar series 'Revisiting Moral Panics: A Critical Examination of 21st Century Social Issues and Anxieties' (ES/J021725/1) between October 2012 and October 2014.

References

Beck, U. (1992) *Risk society: Towards a new modernity*, London: Sage.

Beck, U. (1999) *World risk society*, Cambridge: Polity Press.

Clapton, G. (1993) *Satanic abuse controversy: Social workers and the social work press*, London: University of North London Press.

Cohen, S. (1972) *Folk devils and moral panics: The creation of the mods and rockers*, London: MacGibbon and Kee Ltd.

Cohen, S. (1985) *Visions of social control: Crime, punishment and classification*, Cambridge: Polity Press.

Cohen, S. (1998) *Against criminology,* London: Transaction Publishers.

Cohen, S. (2001) *States of denial knowing about atrocities and suffering*, Cambridge: Polity Press.

Cree, V.E. (2008) 'Confronting sex-trafficking: lessons from history', *International Social Work*, vol 51, no 6, pp 763–76.

Featherstone, B., White, S. and Morris, K. (2014) *Re-imagining child protection: Towards humane social work with families*, Bristol: Policy Press.

Goode, E. and Ben-Yehuda, N. (1994) *Moral panics: The Social construction of deviance*, Oxford: Blackwell.

Hall, S., Critcher, C., Jefferson, T., Clarke, J. and Roberts, B. (1978) *Policing the crisis: Mugging, the state and law and order*, London: Macmillan.

Hunt, A. (1999) *Governing morals: A social history of moral regulation*, Cambridge University Press, New York.

Pearson, G. (1975) *The deviant imagination: Psychiatry, social work and social change*, London: Macmillan.

Pearson, G. (1983) *Hooligan: A history of respectable fears,* London: Macmillan.

Rohloff, A. and Wright, S. (2010) 'Moral panic and social theory: beyond the heuristic', *Current Sociology*, vol 58, no 3, pp 403–19.

Smith, M. (2008) 'Historical abuse in residential child care: an alternative view', *Practice: Social Work in Action*, vol 20, no 1, pp 29–41.

Smith, M. (2010) 'Victim Narratives of historical abuse in residential child care: do we really know what we think we know?', *Qualitative Social Work*, vol 9, no 3, pp 303–20.

Young, J. (1971) *The drugtakers: The social meaning of drug use*, London: Paladin.

Young, J. (2011) *The criminological imagination*, Cambridge: Polity Press

Introduction

Viviene E. Cree

In common with the other bytes in this series, a key theorist within the 'moral panic' genre is introduced here. Stuart Hall's ideas have been pivotal to the development of a more overly political analysis of moral panics. Many of his ideas are reflected in the chapters in this volume and throughout the series, while others have been taken forward in other writing in the field.

Stuart Hall

Stuart McPhail Hall was born on 3 February 1932 in Kingston, Jamaica and first came to the UK in 1951 to study English at Oxford University, after winning a Rhodes scholarship. He described himself as a 'familiar stranger' at Oxford, steeped in English traditions and yet very different socially, culturally and ethnically to the other students and staff. He found politics (Marxism), and became part of the *Universities and Left Review*, which later merged with the *New Reasoner* to form the *New Left Review*, with Hall as its founding editor. Hall completed his MA and began a PhD on the Anglo-American novelist Henry James, before giving up his studies and moving to London, where he worked as a supply teacher in Brixton and a magazine editor. In 1961 he was appointed Lecturer in Film and Media at Chelsea College, London University; in 1964, at the invitation of Richard Hoggart, he moved to the newly formed Centre for Contemporary Cultural Studies (CCCS) at Birmingham University as its first research fellow. He remained until 1979, when he went on to become Professor of Sociology at the Open University, a post that he held until 1998.

Stuart Hall is widely acknowledged as someone who played a significant part in bringing cultural studies from the margins into the centre of academic and public analysis and debate. He collaborated with colleagues in the CCCS on a number of volumes, including *Resistance through Rituals* (1975); *Culture, Media, Language* (1980); *Politics and Ideology* (1986); *The Hard Road to Renewal* (1988); *New Times* (1989); *Critical Dialogues in Cultural Studies* (1996); and *Different: A Historical Context: Contemporary Photographers and Black Identity* (2001). Perhaps his best-known book, *Policing the Crisis. Mugging, the State, and Law and Order* (1978) was a collaboration between academics at the CCCS. The book begins in 1972 with the story of 'a mugging gone wrong' – this was a police officer's description of a street robbery in London that resulted in the death of an elderly widower. Hall and others go on to explore what happened next, including the appropriation of a new scare-word into the British lexicon, that is, 'mugging'. They are at pains to point out that they do not condone street robbery, which they see as a 'manifestation of powerlessness' (1978, p 396). But they argue that the furore around mugging must be understood as a moral panic, focusing as it does on the representation of young, black, working-class men as 'dangerous'. They go on to draw attention to the deliberate focus on 'race' in Thatcherite politics, especially in the characterisation of the 'law and order' agenda. Hall went on to explore this further in *The Politics of Thatcherism* (1983), in which he criticised the Left for making Thatcherism possible because of its traditional statism.

Hall contributed to many non-academic activities during his lifetime. He served on the Runnymede Commission on the Future of Multi-Ethnic Britain between 1997 and 2000; and chaired Autograph (the Association of Black Photographers) and the International Institute of Visual Arts. He helped to secure funding for Rivington Place, in East London, a centre dedicated to public education in multicultural issues.

This series, even without being consciously aware of it, reflects something of the spirit of Stuart Hall, not just in its sceptical approach or its interest in issues of 'race' and class, but because it is interdisciplinary. It tries to 'think outside the box', and is a tribute to Stuart Hall's creativity, imagination and honesty.

Stuart Hall died on 10 February 2014.

Content of this byte

The chapters in this byte all explore, in some way, moral panics and the state. Of course, 'the state' is itself a very broad concept, and therefore it should be no surprise to find chapters here on everything from internet pornography to internet radicalisation, from 'chavs' to 'troubled families', and finally, patient safety. As in the other bytes, authors are writing from different disciplinary backgrounds, though on this occasion all are located in the UK. If there is any consensus across the chapters, it is that moral panics have potentially detrimental consequences for all of us; they can be used by the state, as Hall et al (1978) demonstrated clearly, to justify policies and legislation that are, at the very least, repressive and regressive.

Chapter One, by Jim Greer, tackles a social anxiety that is currently raging across the developed and developing worlds alike, namely, internet pornography and, in particular, the risk of children's access to and use of internet porn. Greer argues that we are all panicking about this, in large part because we hold very contradictory ideas about children, who are at the same time seen both as innocent and naïve and as 'capable of being corrupted'. He argues that the long-term consequences of the crusade against internet pornography are likely to be both censorship and a loss of freedom of speech; he urges that those of us who value the internet's creative and collaborative potential should take note of this now and campaign against it.

The internet remains the focus of concern in Chapter Two, but this time, the subject is the danger of radicalisation through the internet. David McKendrick picks up the story of the murder of off-duty soldier Lee Rigby by two Muslim men on a London street in 2013, an event that was all the more shocking because it (and its aftermath) was filmed by passers-by and the video uploaded to YouTube. McKendrick outlines what he describes as a moral panic that followed this brutal killing as politicians, journalists and policy makers queued up to blame 'cyber jihad' for the murder. This is a story that has echoes of Hall et al's earlier study of 'race' and crime, but the new element of the 'out-of-control' internet adds a new, 21st-century dimension to the panic.

Chapters Three and Four take us in different directions, although both are fundamentally concerned with issues of social class. In Chapter Three, Elias le Grand outlines the creation of the 'chav' stereotype in the UK: the chav is a current-day 'folk devil', young, white, working class and male (there are female chavs, or chavettes, too, often portrayed as pregnant or pushing a pram). The chav is a welfare 'scrounger', a threat to the respectable working class because of their choice to remain unemployed and on benefit. Importantly, le Grand argues that the creation of the chav as folk devil allows the rest of us ('respectable' working-class people and the middle classes) to rest easy in our beds, absolved of any responsibility for increasing poverty levels and inequality in society.

Steve Kirkwood's Chapter Four takes a very different moral panic, although it seems likely that there were some 'chavs' within this story too. He examines the riots that erupted in cities and towns in England during August 2011, following on from the shooting dead of a 29-year-old black man, Mark Duggan, by the police in Tottenham in London. Kirkwood unpicks the process of moral panic as it developed, and asks why it was that the government was able to blame the riots on poor parenting and, most especially, on families without fathers. He argues that the government's focus on 'troubled families' offered a convenient way out – it depoliticised the structural nature of the problems that were brought to a head in the riots in 2011. In that sense, this chapter, perhaps more than any other in this byte, owes allegiance to the work of Stuart Hall and others.

The final chapter considers a very different case-study example of a moral panic, this time the panic around patient safety. William Fear argues that while this might have become a state-led movement, in practice, the campaign for greater patient safety has actually been run from within the medical profession. By retaining an institutional hold on the issue, the medical profession has been able to set the agenda and dictate terms. As a consequence, although vast empires have been built around patient safety, the power of the medical establishment has been reinforced, not undermined. This is an interesting example of what happens when the powerful make use of a moral-panic model for their own ends.

References

Chen, K.-H. and Morley, D. (1996) *Stuart Hall, critical dialogues in cultural studies*, London: Routledge.

Donald, J. and Hall, S. (1986) *Politics and ideology: A reader*, Virginia: Open University Press.

Hall, S. (1988) *The hard road to renewal. Thatcherism and the crisis of the Left*, London: Verso Books.

Hall, S. and Jacques, M. (eds) (1983) *The politics of Thatcherism*, London: Lawrence and Wishart Ltd.

Hall, S. and Jacques, M. (eds) (1989) *New times: Changing face of politics in the 1990s*, London: Lawrence and Wishart Ltd.

Hall, S. and Jefferson, T. (1975; 2nd edn, 2006) *Resistance through rituals: Youth subcultures in post-war Britain* (Cultural Studies Birmingham), London: Routledge.

Hall, S. and Sealy, M. (2001) *Different: A historical context: contemporary photographers and Black identity*, Michigan: University of Michigan Press.

Hall, S., Critcher, C., Jefferson, T., Clarke, J. and R. Bryan (1978; 2nd edn, 2013) *Policing the crisis: Mugging, the state and law and order*, London: Macmillan.

Hall, S., Hobson, R., Lowe, A. and Willis, P. (1980) (2nd edn) *Culture, Media, Language, Trade in Culture, Media, Language: Working Papers in Cultural Studies, 1972–79* (Cultural Studies Birmingham), London: Routledge.

ONE

Children and internet pornography: a moral panic, a salvation for censors and Trojan horse for government colonisation of the digital frontier

Jim Greer

Introduction

This chapter will argue that we are currently experiencing a moral panic around children accessing internet pornography. This issue will be introduced within the context of society's views of young people, echoing previous moral panics about the influence of popular media on children. The chapter will then go on to consider what evidence (if any) exists for the extent of the problem of young people accessing and being influenced by internet pornography. This will be followed by scrutiny of 'moral entrepreneurs', that is, academics and others who are likely to benefit or prosper from internet regulation and the groups and communities who may be collateral damage in the 'war on porn'. Finally, the chapter will evaluate the chances of internet porn initiatives succeeding in their stated aims and the wider implications for society and its relationship with the 'wired worlds' of the internet.

The nature of the panic

On the weekend of 9 and 10 November 2013, the colour supplements of both *The Times* and the *Sunday Times* featured stories about concerns regarding what children do online. *The Times* cover featured a posed shot of a schoolgirl alone in darkened room, her face lit by only her mobile phone, her slightly chilling (or was it fearful?) gaze fixed on the reader. This photograph illustrates well the current moral panic around children and the internet. Children are simultaneously understood to be innocent, yet capable of being corrupted; in control of bewildering technology, yet somehow vulnerable to its dark side; networked to the world, yet also alone and vulnerable. Articles like these have proliferated in print and online media; meanwhile, new scares have been identified and named, including cyberbullying, children sexting, online grooming, adults accessing child pornography and children accessing legal (adult) pornography. These phenomena are often discussed together and almost always interchangeably. The confusion between these issues is evident in, for example, articles that advocate for the use of internet filters to tackle child pornography, when in fact such material is mainly confined to the so-called 'deep web' (Pagliery, 2014).

The relationship with previous moral panics

Concerns about young people and the negative effects of media technology are not new. In the 1950s there was a campaign in the UK against American and 'American-style' comics on the basis of the horrific and violent content they contained. The campaign involved teachers' organisations, women's organisations, trade unions and churches, and, as in the current internet pornography campaign, the evidence that children were being adversely affected was largely anecdotal. In a detailed analysis of the 1950s campaign, Barker (1984a) argued that children were portrayed as innocent on the surface, yet containing a dangerous aspect that could be awoken by exposure to the wrong type of media. This parallels more recent fears about pornography 'distorting [children's] view of sex and relationships' (Cameron, 2013). In common with the current moral panic about children and the internet, strong concern was expressed in the 1950s about long-term damage to children's emotional and psychological development. Barker (1984a) expressed the view that the highly emotive nature of concerns about children's development led to there being no effective opposition to the campaign, and it resulted in the passing of legislation, despite a lack of empirical evidence. The legislation, the Children and Young Persons (Harmful Publications) Act 1955, is still in force.

The 1980s saw another moral panic that focused on children and technology. This time the concern was about children watching violent and horrific films on home video cassettes (so-called 'video nasties'); the rise in recorded crime was blamed on the easy availability of these films (Barker, 1984b). A parliamentary inquiry was quickly organised, the outcome of which was the Video Recordings Act 1984, which made it illegal to sell or distribute most videos without prior censorship by the British Board of Film Classification (BBFC) (Barker, 1984b; Brown, 1984). Barker (1984b, p 2) described the Video Recordings Act as 'the biggest growth in censorship in this country for very many years'.

The extent of the problem

One of the reasons frequently given for concern about young people accessing pornography on the internet is the sheer volume of pornographic websites and web pages that are reputed to exist on the internet. However, there is a lack of reliable information on the amount of pornography on the internet.

One recent attempt to assess what is known about children and their access to pornography is found in the report, *'Basically, Porn is Everywhere': Report of Children's Commissioner: A Rapid Evidence Assessment on the Effect that Access and Exposure to Pornography Has on Children and Young People* (Horvath et al, 2013). This report was commissioned by the Office of the Children's Commissioner (OCC) in England as part of its Inquiry into Child Sexual Exploitation in Gangs and Groups (CSEGG). The study was limited in time and scope (as its title suggests) and was based mainly on a literature review of published papers, very few of which were from the UK. Nevertheless, the report does contain some findings that are instructive. Most notably, the report found very little research anywhere on the effects on children and young people of exposure to pornography. It points out that comparable research on the effects on children of violence in the media elicits contradictory evidence. The report states (Horvath et al, 2013, p 51) that 'For every study which concludes that viewing violence causes aggression in young people, there seems to be one which contradicts this.' The report raises concerns about the ethics of trying to look for causal relationships between exposure to pornography and harm and suggests that future research should consider questions such as: 'what are young people seeing when they are exposed to pornography?' and 'what roles do culture and socialisation play ... on young people's attitudes to pornography?' The report also looked at evidence in relation to children, the media and sex. One study found that the mass media explained only 13% of variance when looking at young people's attitudes towards sex; parents, religion, peers, grades at school and demographic factors were equally influential (L'Engle et al, 2004). Another study found a correlation between the amount of sexually explicit media consumed by boys and an increased tendency to see women as sex objects (Peter and Valkenburg, 2007). However, the report concluded that sexual stereotyping is not necessarily indicative of how young people view their relationships, or of their actual behaviour. Looking at the picture overall, there was little to justify the title '*Basically Porn is Everywhere*' or to justify David Cameron (2013) in proposing that internet service providers should install 'default on' internet filtering in every household. Rather, the report recommends that the Department for Education needs to drive improvement of sex and relationships education, including an awareness of pornography (recommendations 1–3) and that the government has to increase parents' awareness of their responsibilities towards children in this area (recommendation 4).

So why has the threat to children from internet porn captured popular and political attention?

One possible reason for the popular and political attention on the threat to children from internet porn is the cascade effect (Kuran and

Sunstein, 1999), in which media attention creates public interest, which in turn creates more media attention. Media attention in this way feeds the availability heuristic (Tversky and Kahneman, 1974), by which people will over-estimate the size of risks that are easier to bring into recall. Another reason, identified by Boyd and Marwick (2009), is that technology makes risky behaviours 'more conspicuous'. Sexting and accessing pornography leave a trail in ways that behaviours like 'show me yours and I'll show you mine' wouldn't. Furthermore, the way in which an issue is framed affects how it is perceived (Tversky and Kahneman, 1986). Most of the discussions in the UK media about children and internet pornography (see, for example, Orr, 2013) have been framed in terms of how we can protect children, rather than how we can maintain the educational and political benefits of free access to the internet.

As with the previous moral panics of horror comics and video nasties, the emotive nature of the issue has silenced debate; any potential loss of freedom of speech seems to us a small price to pay in comparison with something as serious as children and children's moral development.

Cultural differences in how much value is given to free speech and free expression play a role. In general, the British media's reporting of the issue has lacked any real defence of free speech, with even liberal media such as the *Guardian*'s website running opinion pieces in favour of internet filters (for example, Orr, 2013). By contrast, US reporting on UK internet filtering has focused on freedom of speech issues (for example, the *New York Times* commentary by Ong, 2013)) and lampooning of the UK establishment (for example, an American liberal video podcast which had David Cameron portrayed as a Town Crier (The Young Turks, 2013). Sunstein (2005) argues that it is widely believed that Europe operates from a precautionary principle in relation to risk, whereas in the US there is a normally held to be a need for evidence of harm before risks will be regulated for. However, Sunstein adds that this can be seen as an over-generalisation and that the US and Europe differ in the types of risk that are perceived to be greatest. In the UK, the very possibility that children may be being harmed by pornography is enough to justify the use of governmental directives. As Furedi writes: 'While many of the moral transgressions of the past have lost significance, those directed at children are policed more intensively than at any time in human history' (Furedi, 2013, p 45). Thus, the topic of children and internet pornography brings together two contemporary areas of fear – the fear of novel technology out of control and the fear of harm to children.

Claims makers/moral entrepreneurs

Government policy on children and the internet was taken forward by the Conservative MP Clare Perry via an *Independent Parliamentary Inquiry into Online Child Protection* (Perry, 2012). Despite the title, this inquiry did not focus, as we might have expected, on online grooming, abuse or bullying, but instead looked at children's internet consumption and the need to filter it. The report was also not, as the title suggests, 'independent'. Instead, it was (as stated on the report), sponsored by Premiere Christian Media (a UK Christian broadcaster and campaigning charity) in partnership Safer Media for a Safer Society (a charity 'seeking to reduce the harmful effects of the media on our children, families and society'), two organisations with a clear vested interest in promoting a climate of concern around the effects of online media.

The key findings of the report included the fact that most parents did not use existing filters because they trusted their children to use the internet safely and responsibly. Furthermore, parents who did use filters were more concerned with filtering suicide sites than pornography. This could have been seen as a positive reflection on the character of the nation's children and the trust that their parents have in them. However, the report recommended that internet service providers (ISPs) should be instructed to roll out internet filters to all homes, supported by legislation if necessary. Following Perry's review, the Department for Education in England was tasked with carrying out a wider consultation on how internet filters might be rolled out. The findings of that consultation (Department for Education, 2013) were that a majority of parents who took part felt that child internet safety was a shared responsibility between parents and ISPs, not government, and that a majority did not want any of the filtering options on offer. Despite this, David Cameron decided to go ahead with a requirement for 'default on' filtering. The filtering systems that are to be introduced in the UK require citizens (irrespective of whether they have children or not) to make an active decision to turn these filters off. A failure to respond to an online prompt will result in the filters being set at 'on'. The account holder is then presented with a menu of categories that they can have filtered out. It seems likely that the 'default on' approach will place psychological pressure to accept the filters through what Kahneman, Knetsch and Thaler (1991) have termed 'status quo bias'; someone will accept the default setting because it is a suggestion/recommendation by the policy maker, who may be seen as an expert. Parents may also be concerned about being identified as someone who is an irresponsible parent or perhaps as someone who is interested in terrorism or pornography. They may be concerned that their filtering choices may become known to the authorities or be 'leaked' onto the web, or have negative consequences for them if they were ever suspected of any kind of offence, abuse or neglect in relation to children.

The House of Commons Culture, Media and Sport Committee's report on *Online Safety* (2014, section 4.87) asserts that the internet is currently a 'free for all' in which anyone with a computer could be a publisher. The unstated implication is that this is an unsatisfactory state of affairs that needs to be curbed. This theme is echoed in the Department for Culture, Media and Sport (2013) policy paper, *Connectivity, Content and Consumers: Britain's Digital Platform for Growth*. This document again has a strong emphasis on 'consumer safety', signalling a policy direction that, I would argue, represents a move towards government colonisation and control of the internet: rather than being common land where international citizens can share ideas and collaborate freely and take part in free commerce, the internet is to be controlled by national governments. Censorship bodies such as the BBFC and the Authority for Television on Demand (ATVOD), who feared that the internet would make them redundant, are now waiting for their share of the regulatory bonanza that fears about children and pornography seem likely to open up. The ATVOD has recently issued its own 'research report' (ATVOD, 2014). Page 15 has large banner text stating that '44,000 children aged 6–11 visited an adult website from a PC or a laptop in December 2013'. However, a footnote in tiny writing on the same page states that 'these demographics do not meet minimum sample size standards'. Reporting of the ATVOD report has tended to focus on the alarmist headline findings, rather than notes of methodological caution. ATVOD's strong presence seems likely to increase as we move ahead and the regulator seeks to increase its role in online protection.

The wider implications of the panic for social work and wider society

There is much to fear from a closed, regulated internet for social work and for those who are concerned about the rights of oppressed people all around the world. The policy of 'default on' internet filtering has already caused damage, because filtering programmes are relatively unsophisticated and cannot distinguish between harmful material and educational or informative material. There have been examples of access to LGBT information sites being lost (Cooper, 2013), and also of access to sex education and sexual health websites being curtailed (Blake, 2013). There is also a danger that access to sites that carry independent news and information on issues such as global affairs and terrorism, female genital mutilation, abuse and human trafficking, forced prostitution and so on will be closed off. It is possible to ask for blocked sites to be 'white listed'. However, it is not clear how easy this process might be and people may not realise that they want to access a site if they cannot see what is on it in the first place. Young people who wish to access information about concerns such as anorexia may also find access blocked to sites that would actually be helpful to them. Teenagers who want to discuss issues to do with relationships can easily have their access to these sites curtailed if their parents deny household access to web forums.

For those who care about child protection issues such as online grooming, exploitation and cyberbullying, internet filtering gives the illusion that the government is doing something to protect children online, when in fact it isn't addressing these problems. Of course, there will be a small number of young people who may become hooked into watching online porn, just as a small number will become addicted to gambling or other potentially harmful activities. Some children and young people may see things online that are at the very least unattractive, if not downright abusive. But Ferguson (2014) suggests that we should think about the relationship between the media and consumers as an interactive, rather than a passive one (the young person is as much 'doing' as being 'done to'). Furthermore, if a young person is spending a lot of time accessing online pornography, then they probably have wider problems that would exist even if pornography was not available to them in this way.

Conclusion

Early results from the roll-out of filters are that uptake has been poor, despite the 'default on' approach. An Ofcom (2014) report on the level of activation of filters by new internet account customers is 5% for BT, 8% for Sky, 36% for TalkTalk and 4% for Virgin. The low take-up by Virgin customers has been partly explained by engineers' installation by-passing the option and not giving customers the choice to activate filters at installation. It is perhaps not surprising that the overall take-up is so low, in the light of previous public consultation on the issue. However, it will be interesting to see whether the government will accept that the public has responded negatively to network-level filtering as an option, or whether this will be seen as a justification for forcing families without children to use filters.

Another recent piece of legislation, the Data Retention and Investigatory Powers Act 2014, has been passed amid claims by technology law experts that it has been 'unnecessarily rushed through Parliament' and 'represents a serious expansion of surveillance' (Kiss, 2014). The 'video nasties' moral panic was associated with fears that violent media in a new technology could fuel civil unrest and crime as well as corrupting children. The existing moral panic again plays of fears about new technology, corruption of childhood and a new threat of violence – this time from terrorism and religious extremism, as will be discussed more fully in subsequent chapters.

Government regulation and control of the internet could lead to legal and financial barriers to both the publication and consumption of information. For those who value the capacity of the internet to offer an unfettered space for protest, minority views and the challenging the powerful interests, this is a discomforting direction of travel for government policy.

For social workers who are concerned about the risks to children from new technologies there are plenty of alternatives to censorship, as demonstrated by Childline's (2014) 'Zipit' app, which enables young people to send smart retorts to close down sexting or requests by phone for inappropriate photographs. Initiatives like these offer a child-centred alternative to blanket internet censorship.

References

ATVOD (2014) *For Adults Only? A Research Report by the Authority for Television on Demand*, 28 March 2014, www.atvod.co.uk/uploads/files/For_Adults_Only_FINAL.pdf.

Barker, M. (1984a) *A haunt of fears: The strange history of the British Horror Comics campaign*, London: Pluto Press.

Barker, M. (1984b) 'Nasty politics or video nasties', in M. Barker (ed) *The video nasties: Freedom and censorship in the media*, London: Pluto Press, pp 7–38.

Blake, S. (2013) 'Porn or better sex education', www.pinknews.co.uk/2013/08/21/comment-porn-or-better-sex-education/ (accessed 17 March 2013)

Boyd, D. and Marwick, A. (2009) 'The conundrum of visibility', *Journal of Children and Media*, vol 3, no 4, pp 410–14.

Brown, B. (1984) 'Exactly what we wanted', in M. Barker (ed) *The video nasties: Freedom and censorship in the media*, London: Pluto Press, pp 68–87.

Cameron, D. (2013) 'The Internet and pornography: Prime Minister Calls for Action', speech, 24 July, www.gov.uk/government/speeches/the-internet-and-pornography-prime-minister-calls-for-action (accessed 17 March 2015).

Childline (2014) Zipit app, www.childline.org.uk/Play/GetInvolved/Pages/sexting-zipit-app.aspx.

Cooper, C. (2013) 'David Cameron's plan for internet-porn filters "risks hurting LGBT community"', *Independent* (21 August), www.independent.co.uk/news/uk/politics/david-camerons-plan-for-internetporn-filters-risks-hurting-lgbt-community-8778956.html .

Department for Culture, Media and Sport (2013) *Connectivity, Content and Consumers: Britain's digital platform for growth*, https://www.gov.uk/government/publications/connectivity-content-and-consumers-britains-digital-platform-for-growth.

Department for Education (2013) *The Government Response to the Consultation on Parental Internet Controls*, http://webarchive.nationalarchives.gov.uk/20130903121526/http:/media.education.gov.uk/assets/files/pdf/c/20130122%20gov%20response%20to%20parental%20internet%20controls.pdf.

Ferguson, C. (2014) 'Is video game violence bad?', *The Psychologist*, vol 21, no 5, pp 324–7.

Furedi, F. (2013) *Moral crusades in an age of mistrust: The Jimmy Savile scandal*, Basingstoke: Palgrave Macmillan.

Horvath, M.A.H., Alys, L., Massey, K., Pina, A., Scally, M. and Adler, J.R. (2013) *'Basically, porn is everywhere': A rapid evidence assessment on the effect that access and exposure to pornography has on children and young people*, London: Children's Commissioner.

House of Commons Culture Media and Sport Committee (2014) *Online Safety*, 6th report of session 2013–14, www.publications.parliament.uk/pa/cm201314/cmselect/cmcumeds/729/72902.htm.

Kahneman, D., Knetsch, J.L. and Thaler, R.H. (1991) 'Anomalies: the endowment effect, loss aversion, and status quo bias', *Journal of Economic Perspectives*, vol 5, no 1, pp 193–206.

Kiss, J. (2014) 'Academics: UK "Drip" data law changes are "serious expansion of surveillance"', *Guardian* (15 July), www.theguardian.com/technology/2014/jul/15/academics-uk-data-law-surveillance-bill-rushed-parliament.

Kuran, T. and Sunstein, C. (1999) 'Availability cascades and risk regulation', *Stanford Law Review*, vol 51, pp 683–768.

legislation.gov.uk (2014) Data Retention and Investigatory Powers Act 2014, www.legislation.gov.uk/ukpga/2014/27/contents/enacted.

L'Engle, K.L., Brown, J.D. and Kenneavy, K. (2004) 'The mass media as an important context for adolescents' sexual behaviour', *Journal of Adolescent Health*, vol 38 pp 186–92.

Ofcom (2014) *Report on Internet Safety Measures*, July 2014.

Ong, J. (2013) 'Internet Filtering Should be "Opt –In"', *New York Times* (19 August), www.nytimes.com/roomfordebate/2013/08/19/can-free-speech-and-internet-filters-co-exist/internet-filtering-should-be-opt-in.

Orr, D. (2013) 'Why such outrage over porn filters ? The idea seems perfectly reasonable to me', *Guardian* (26 July), www.theguardian.com/commentisfree/2013/jul/26/why-such-outrage-porn-filters (accessed 17 March 2015).

Pagliery, J. (2014) 'The Deep Web you don't know about', http://money.cnn.com/2014/03/10/technology/deep-web/ (accessed 17 March 2015).

Perry, C. (2012) 'Premiere Christian Media and Safer Media for a Safer Society', *Independent Parliamentary Inquiry into Online Child Protection*, www.claireperry.org.uk/downloads/independent-parliamentary-inquiry-into-online-child-protection.pdf.

Peter, J. and Valkenburg, P.M. (2007) 'Adolescents' exposure to a sexualized media environment and their notions of women as sex objects', *Sex Roles*, vol 56, pp 381–95.

Sunday Times (2013) Colour magazine, 10 November.

Sunstein, C.R. (2005) 'Precautions against what? The availability heuristic and cross-cultural risk perception', *Alabama Law Review*, vol 75, pp 2–3.

The Young Turks (2013) 'Internet porn blocked all over Britain', https://www.youtube.com/watch?v=ACrrGTiV1VI 2013 (accessed 6 February 2015).

Times (2013) Colour magazine, 9 November.

Tversky, A. and Kahneman, D. (1974) 'Judgement under uncertainty: heuristics and biases', *Science*, vol 185, pp 1124–31.

Tversky, A. and Kahneman, D. (1986) 'Rational choice and framing of decisions', *Journal of Business*, vol 59, no 4, pp 251–78.

TWO

Internet radicalisation and the 'Woolwich Murder'

David McKendrick

Introduction

Lee Rigby was murdered in London on 22 May 2013. He was returning to the army barracks in Woolwich where he was living when he was hit by a car and then murdered by two men wielding knives and a cleaver. This event took place in broad daylight on a busy street in the capital city. The brutality of the murder seemed incomprehensible, as was the apparent randomness of the attack: Lee Rigby was targeted because he was a soldier – his attackers knew nothing more about him. They even took time after the assault to talk to passers-by, some of whom recorded the interaction on their mobile phones before uploading the footage to social networking sites, including YouTube. Both men were subsequently shot and wounded by armed police officers and taken to hospital. In February 2014, Michael Adebolajo and Michael Adebowale were found guilty of murder and given sentences of whole-life and 45 years, respectively. Video footage of the event was used repeatedly by the mainstream media after the murder and again at the time of the trial, bringing a 'real time' dimension to the attack and increasing its shock value considerably. An anti-Muslim backlash erupted in various parts of the UK in 2013 and 2014, with a series of assaults on mosques and on men and women assumed to be Muslim.

It is not surprising, given the seriousness and the unexpected nature of this event, that there has been intense speculation as to why it might have happened, and what might be done to prevent it happening again. A familiar story has emerged, picked up and carried in all of the major news outlets, that the attackers had been 'radicalised on the internet', supporting a narrative of the internet as a place where extreme views are contained and where people who harbour vicious, murderous intent have a safe and secure home. The internet, and more specifically social media channels such as YouTube, Twitter and Facebook, are portrayed here as the sites through which vulnerable young men (and women) are radicalised. The phrase 'cyber jihad' has been coined to describe aspects of internet activity. At the same time, Lee Rigby's murder was used to strengthen the argument for the passing of a Communications Data Bill aimed at giving the police and others more powers to investigate citizens' use of the internet, the so-called 'Snoopers' Charter'. Although this Bill failed to progress in Parliament, a subsequent Act was rushed through in July 2014, the Data Retention and Investigatory Powers Act 2014 (also discussed in Chapter One).

Radicalisation and the internet

It is important now to take a step back from this and to ask: what is going on here? Should we view Lee Rigby's murder as part of a wider campaign of terror or as an isolated, horrific event? In seeking explanation and understanding of the event in Woolwich, there is a natural desire to seek to distance it from ourselves and our everyday lives. The remote nature of the internet provides a ready vehicle for this: we can reassure ourselves that, lurking somewhere deep in the shadows of the internet, social media channels exist where young, disenfranchised minority groups become 'radicalised' (a few years ago we might have called it 'brainwashed'). By creating this spectre that empowers our 'folk devils' (Cohen, 1972), we create a comfort space between ourselves and their actions. In other words, developing a narrative of 'extremism' means that you have decreased responsibility for the actions and motivations of the extremist. Your safety is secure. But is it? Or is it more likely that the reaction to extreme events like this may actually lead to a worse (and less safe) situation for all of us, as classic moral panic theory suggests? History shows us that moral panics about religious extremism are nothing new; the current social anxiety about young radical men is also familiar because it reminds us of earlier moral panics centred on the behaviour of young people (Cohen, 1972; Pearson, 1983; Thompson, 1998).

To help us think this through more carefully it might be helpful to look at the government's policy on radicalisation. Classic moral panic theory requires the participation of 'claims makers', those who would seek to claim relationships between issues or events that are unrelated, which then stokes fear over a particular subject in order to support a particular agenda, often their own. This can be achieved by stealth, through associating fear of particularly extreme behaviour with more general everyday concerns. In this particular case, the then Conservative Minister for Security, James Brokenshire (now Immigration Minister), in a speech on 27 June 2013 described what he saw as a link between internet radicalisation, terrorism and the government's initiatives for supporting children and families in difficulty:

> One particular interest of mine is the importance of ensuring that our counter radicalisation strategy sits alongside other key areas of public sector work … I think it's important that we articulate our counter radicalisation strategy within the context of safeguarding … In a similar vein, I am keen to ensure that the Government's work to support troubled families is aligned to our work to support vulnerable individuals at risk of being drawn into terrorist activity. (Brokenshire, 2013)

The counter-radicalisation strategy being discussed here is CONTEST (HM Government, 2011), a wide-ranging strategy that sought to provide an 'end to end' approach to tackling the issue of terrorism, radicalisation in general and, specifically, internet radicalisation. The four strands to the strategy are outlined here:

- pursue: to stop terrorist attacks
- prevent: to stop people becoming terrorists or supporting terrorism

- protect: to strengthen our protection against a terrorist attack
- prepare: to mitigate the impact of a terrorist attack.

The Prevent section of the strategy aimed to challenge the development of radicalisation in local communities by providing financial support for community projects in particular areas where the government had identified there being a risk of radicalisation. (It is of interest to note that the word 'terrorism' features heavily in the title of the document and not 'radicalism' or 'radicalisation'; the emphasis is plainly on terrorism.) Community projects such as these would work in areas that the government had identified as being at increased risk of radicalisation; social workers, nurses and teachers were to be in the 'front line' of the strategy to counter radicalisation. Prevent was initially developed in 2005 as part of the government's CONTEST strategy, following the London bombings. It underwent a number of revisions in 2011 and 2013 but it remains the government's primary social policy for challenging any form of domestic terrorism and extremism.

Perhaps unsurprisingly, there has been significant criticism of the approach taken in both Prevent and Channel. In 2009, the Institute of Race Relations first published Kundnani's *Spooked: How Not To Prevent Violent Extremism*, an evaluation of the strategy, which argued that this was overly focused on Muslim communities and was an attempt to insert counter-terrorist police officers into communities where there was a high Muslim population. *Spooked*, and a follow-up article in 2011 entitled 'Still Spooked', argued that the approach targeted vulnerable populations such as young Muslims and saw them through a lens of 'at risk of radicalisation'. Moreover, the monies and resources provided to develop preventative and diversionary services were decided at a central government level with little or no communication with the local areas where they were to be delivered. Because of this, the strategy never engaged effectively with the populations it aimed to support and local communities felt that there was an unprecedented level of intrusion into their daily lives.

Spooked also took issue with the characterisation in Prevent and Channel of radical and extreme views as inevitably dangerous, as if holding radical views meant that you were automatically a risk to others. The danger inherent in such an attitude is that simply holding radical views becomes something that requires a response from counter-terrorist police officers and other government agencies that seek to reduce and challenge domestic terrorism. This securitisation of those who hold radical views has been criticised as stifling and undermining fundamental democratic rights to free speech; by making the link between extremism and terrorism explicit in this way, the state gives permission for greater surveillance of increased numbers of the population and gradually advances itself into the private lives of citizens. The strategy also runs the risk of driving away from the democratic process the very young people that it purports to wish to engage with. As *Spooked* identified, the social and economic factors in people's lives that may contribute to a sense of isolation, anger and frustration are largely ignored, as the dominant emphasis is on significant risk to society that gives permission for the state to act in increasingly severe ways.

While *Spooked* focused on the experiences of young Muslim people in respect of the strategy, there is a further concern that should be explored. The strategy seeks to identify radicalism across the spectrum of 'troubled families' and 'safeguarding', thus affecting all countries of the UK, because counter-terrorism is a reserved Westminster power. The Troubled Families programme (TFP) is described thus:

> The aim of the programme is to 'turn round' the lives of the 120,000 most troubled and 'troublesome' families in the UK, by the end of the current Parliament in May 2015. Troubled families are defined nationally as those who commit crime and/or anti-social behaviour, whose children are not attending school, and where at least one adult is on out of work benefits. If a family meets all three of these criteria they are classified as a 'troubled family', although the figure of 120,000 originally came from research looking at the extent of multiple disadvantages and not 'problematic behaviours'. (Levitas, 2012)

Local authorities, who are tasked with implementing the programme, can use 'local filter criteria' if a family meets two out of the three criteria. The TFP operates on a payment-by-results basis, where local authorities 'claim' payments from central government once they have achieved certain milestones relating to the family's behaviour and/or labour market participation. The programme was voted the 'top government policy in a poll of local authority chief executive officers' in 2013 (Department for Communities and Local Government, 2013).

> 'Safeguarding' has an even broader definition:
>
> * protecting children from maltreatment
> * preventing impairment of children's health or development
> * ensuring that children are growing up in circumstances consistent with the provision of safe and effective care
> * taking action to enable all children and young people to have the best outcome.
>
> [...] the action we take to promote the welfare of children and protect them from harm – is everyone's responsibility. Everyone who comes into contact with children and families has a role to play. (HM Government, 2009)

If Prevent and Channel are delivered through the prism of universal services that engage with all members of the community, this locates the risk of radicalisation, and indeed of domestic terrorism, in the widest possible arena; the net to challenge terrorism and radicalisation is now wide enough to include everyone within it. The Channel literature makes this abundantly clear:

> *Channel* uses existing collaboration between local authorities, statutory partners (such as the education and health sectors, social services, children's and youth services

and offender management services), the police and the local community to:

- identify individuals at risk of being drawn into terrorism
- assess the nature and extent of that risk
- develop the most appropriate support plan for the individuals concerned.

Channel is about safeguarding children and adults from being drawn into committing terrorist-related activity. It is about early intervention to protect and divert people away from the risk they face before illegality occurs. (HM Government, 2012)

These are powerful concepts. Equating 'early intervention' – a service seen as benign and supportive and that aims to support vulnerable people in a manner that negates the need for further statutory intervention – with prevention of terrorist attacks that threaten the fabric of society inserts the most restrictive elements of the state into services that are seen as offering support and encouragement to vulnerable families.

Deviancy amplification

The idea of deviancy amplification is at the heart of moral panic literature (see Cohen, 1972; Young, 1971). Writing as far back as 1964, the sociologist Leslie Wilkins introduced the concept of deviancy amplification. Wilkins argued that deviancy amplification was a deliberate strategy to exaggerate small individual acts of deviance and to amplify them in order to support a wider set of goals – goals that sought to label increasingly wider groups within society as being risky or concerning. In so doing, the existing powers maintained their position and were able to justify increasingly restrictive and intrusive responses. State hegemony was thereby secured, using the various instruments of the state (in this case, public services, the police and the intelligence service) and by the effective use of deviancy amplification. Brokenshire's earlier comments can be seen as classic deviancy amplification tactics; they have led not only to a securitisation of social policy but to an increased emphasis on securitising public servants, particularly when this is considered in respect of safeguarding or the TFP. To support this, the evidence of interventions under Prevent and Channel makes for interesting reading. In *Still Spooked,* we discover that:

> According to Freedom of Information Act requests submitted to the twelve police forces involved in Channel, 1,120 individuals were identified by Channel project practitioners as on a pathway to radicalisation between 2007 and 2010. Of these, 290 were under sixteen years old and fifty-five were under 12. Over 90 per cent were Muslim; the rest were identified for potential involvement in far-right extremism. Of these 1,120 individuals, 286 were deemed to be in need of a further intervention of some kind. (Kundnani, 2011)

There is a stark difference between the 286 who are seen as requiring 'further intervention' and the widest possible number of children known through the TFP, safeguarding and early intervention. There is a lack of analysis as to why these young people have come to be at risk of radicalisation; ordinary life events such as adolescence, transitions, the death of a loved one or indeed the general trials and tribulations that we all experience as part of daily experiences can cause us to think differently about life and can lead to decision making that would not otherwise be considered if the conditions we find ourselves in change in an unexpected or damaging way.

In this sense, the notion of 'internet radicalisation' can be understood as a classic moral panic. Similar to Cohen's original 1972 work, the focus is once more on young people who are cast as 'folk devils'. The 'claims makers' in this case are the state, specifically the minister James Brokenshire, and deviancy amplification is used to perpetuate the ruling cultural hegemony, by subjugating those whom it has labelled as being at risk of radicalisation. The inherent danger is that we concentrate our efforts on the concept of radicalisation without developing an acute understanding of the other factors that are at play. The work of Stuart Hall (1975, 1978, 1980) is especially instructive here.

To return to Lee Rigby's murder. Latour (1993) suggests that to understand people, we must place them in their networks – that is, in the social, political, economic and technological world that they inhabit and interact with. On the YouTube footage, we hear the explanation/justification of one of the attackers as he rails against government policy, war, bombing of countries, racial and religious intolerance and the anger of young people. He clearly locates his actions in a network, which he understands in his own unique way. To get close to understanding his actions, we need to understand his network, in all its complexity and all its brutality. The young people targeted through the Prevent policy have similarly complex, but presumably very different, networks, each one navigating their own way through them, often in typically excessive teenage ways. Some of them will be drawn towards extremism; however, the deliberately engineered proximity of extremism, radicalism and terrorism draws them into a securitised world of threat and danger. Adolescents are at a formative stage in their life, and many are beginning to experiment with the content of the adult world. It is a time of exploration and discovery and a time when young people are influenced by the complex content of the networks they are a part of. As moral panic theory suggests, if we view the experiences of young people through a narrow paradigm of radicalisation and extremism we may increase the danger we are exposed to by failing to take into account the diversity of their lived experience. Narrow populist responses, often inflated by the media, can contribute to young people's feeling excluded or alienated and can encourage them to seek others who feel the same. While the reality for some young people may be that they are attracted to extremist views, this should not prompt a response that sees them as either 'at risk' or worse still 'a risk'; we need to have mechanisms that see young people in their fullest, most global sense and appreciate the complexities that make them so. If we are seeking to reduce risk and danger while encouraging a more nurturing, caring and understanding environment, we need to develop a more holistic understanding of young people and the issues they are facing.

I would like to suggest that the internet is only one potential aspect of the young person's network; it is akin to suggesting that publishers are responsible for what happens after people read books, or that violent films lead to violent actions. This is a dangerous path: content is not created by the medium; rather, content is created, in this case, by the actions, thoughts and beliefs of human beings. It may well then be conveyed in a variety of mediums, but the crucial point is that the vehicle is a container for the message that is created by the thoughts, feelings and opinions of individuals. This then interacts with the networks of individual actors in a similarly complicated journey, in a process that we must try to understand in all of its unique, multifaceted complexity. The true extent of any part played by the internet in the terrible crime committed at Woolwich has yet to emerge; only then can we learn the lessons that it will offer us.

References

Brokenshire, J. (2013) 'Countering violent extremism through communications', speech to the Global Counter Terrorism Forum (27 June), https://www.gov.uk/government/speeches/security-minister-james-brokenshire-countering-violent-extremism-through-communications (accessed 6 February 2015).

Cohen, S. (1972) *Folk Devils and Moral Panics*, London: MacGibbon & Kee.

Department for Communities and Local Government (2013) 'Troubled Families programme receives extra £200 million boost', www.gov.uk/government/news/troubled-families-programme-receives-extra-200-million-boost (accessed 17 March 2013).

Hall, S. and Jefferson, T. (1975; 2nd edn 2006) *Resistance through rituals: Youth subcultures in post-war Britain* (Cultural Studies Birmingham), London: Routledge.

Hall, S., Critcher, C., Jefferson, T., Clarke, J. and R. Bryan (1978; 2nd edn 2013) *Policing the Crisis: Mugging, the State and Law and Order*, London: Macmillan.

Hall, S., Hobson, R., Lowe, A. and Willis, P. (1980) (2nd edn) *Culture, Media, Language, Trade in Culture, Media, Language: Working Papers in Cultural Studies, 1972–79* (Cultural Studies Birmingham), London: Routledge.

HM Government (2009) *Working Together to Safeguard Children Consultation Document, A guide to inter-agency working to safeguard and promote the welfare of children* (December), https://www.education.gov.uk/consultations/downloadableDocs/Working%20Together%20to%20Safeguard%20ChildrenV2.pdf.

HM Government (2011) *CONTEST: The United Kingdom's Strategy for Countering Terrorism* (July), https://www.gov.uk/government/uploads/system/uploads/attachment_data/file/97994/contest-summary.pdf.

HM Government (2011) *Prevent Strategy* (June), Cm 8092, https://www.gov.uk/government/uploads/system/uploads/attachment_data/file/97976/prevent-strategy-review.pdf.

HM Government (2012) *Channel: Protecting vulnerable people from being drawn into terrorism: A guide for local partnerships* (October), https://www.gov.uk/government/uploads/system/uploads/attachment_data/file/118194/channel-guidance.pdf.

Kundnani, A. (2009) *Spooked: How not to prevent violent extremism*, Institute of Race Relations, www.irr.org.uk/publications/issues/spooked-how-not-to-prevent-violent-extremism/.

Kundnani, A. (2011) 'Still Spooked; How Not To Prevent Violent Extremism', Institute of Race Relations, www.irr.org.uk/news/still-spooked/.

Latour, B. (1993) *We have never been modern*, trans. C. Porter, Boston, MA: Harvard University Press.

Levitas, R. (2012) 'There may be "trouble" ahead: what we know about those 120,000 "troubled" families', www.poverty.ac.uk/sites/default/files/attachments/WP%20Policy%20Response%20No.3-%20%20%27Trouble%27%20ahead%20%28Levitas%20Final%2021April2012%29.pdf (accessed 17 March 2015).

Pearson, G. (1983) *Hooligan: A history of respectable fears*, Basingstoke: Macmillan.

Thompson, K. (1998) *Moral panics*, London: Routledge.

Wilkins, L. (1964) *Social deviance*, London: Routledge & Kegan Paul.

Young, J. (1971) *The drugtakers: The social meaning of drug use,* London: Paladin.

THREE

Moralising discourse and the dialectical formation of class identities: the social reaction to 'chavs' in Britain

Elias le Grand

Introduction

> They are the non-respectable working-classes: the dole-scroungers, petty criminals, football hooligans and teenage pram-pushers. (Lewis, 2004).

Since the early 2000s, the 'chav' has become a widely spread stereotype, well-institutionalised into British public and everyday discourse (le Grand, 2013). The term is tied to strong forms of hostility and moral-aesthetic distinction, and commonly applied to white working-class youths appropriating a certain style of appearance, including what is known as 'streetwear' clothing and jewellery. Drawing on an analysis of news media, websites and popular culture, this chapter discusses the social reaction to chavs and how it is bound up with the formation of class identities.

Following calls to extend the conceptual reach of moral panic analysis (Hier, 2002, 2008, 2011; Critcher, 2009, 2013; Hier et al, 2011; Hunt, 2011), I conceptualise moral panic as a strong and volatile type of social reaction rooted in long-term processes of moral regulation. Both moral panic and moral regulation are conceived as moralisation processes that entail the formation of moralising discourses that act upon the conduct of both self and other. Moralisation therefore involves a dialectical relationship between those actors who moralise certain issues and those who are the object of such moralising discourses and practices.

However, Critcher (2009) states that while moral panic discourses focus on constructing the 'folk devil' as a threat to the moral order and an object of social control measures, moral regulation projects typically involve processes of moral governance, or the reformation of 'character' or the adaptation of behaviour.

In this chapter, I explore the ways in which such dialectical processes of moralisation are tied to the formation of class identities, and to this end I draw on a multi-dimensional, relational notion of class informed by Bourdieu (1984 [1979], 1986, 1987). Bourdieu argues that classed forms of identification and distinction are tied to individuals' unequal access to economic, cultural and social capital; individuals from different classed social locations have differing possibilities to construct identities that are valued and recognised in society. Class formation is therefore tied to hierarchies of moral worth (Skeggs, 1997; Sayer, 2005).

The social reaction to chavs

The emergence and diffusion of the chav stereotype in many ways follows that of a classic moral panic. The term appeared suddenly, 'as if from nowhere', at the beginning of the 20th century. In particular, the 'humorous' website Chavscum, set up in December 2003, was instrumental in constructing and diffusing images of chavs on the internet. By the beginning of 2004, news media caught on and soon chavs were all over the public realm. A LexisNexis database search of the term 'chav' in the 16 UK newspapers with nationwide distribution shows that there were no mentions of the term in 2003, but in 2004 it was mentioned in 374 articles. The same year it also became a dictionary term and was named the buzzword of the year (Dent, 2004). The term 'chav' has continued to be used in news media. In 2013, as many as 481 newspaper articles mentioned the term. It can therefore be argued that the term has been well institutionalised into British public discourse.

Like many moral panics, however, the phenomenon over which the social reaction emerged has existed for much longer. Young working-class people in streetwear clothing associated with low social status and loutish behaviour have existed throughout the UK since the 1990s (Hayward and Yar, 2006). Moreover, the term 'chav' has been used in South-East England since at least the 1970s, although it was not tied any particular group of youths and largely lacked derogatory meanings (for a discussion of the origins of the term, see le Grand, 2010).

The chav as folk devil

In public discourse, chavs have frequently been the object of moral outrage, ridicule and disgust. The image of the chav is largely constructed through practices of consumption (Hayward and Yar, 2006) and often denotes poverty and deprivation. Chavs are said to live on council estates and to gather in gangs, occupying public spaces such as street corners, shopping centres and McDonald's restaurants. They smoke, binge drink and live on a diet of cheap and unhealthy food, especially fast food. In general, the appearance and lifestyles of chavs are coded as excessive, hedonistic, unhealthy, wasteful and vulgar. For instance, the *Telegraph* sneers at chavs' style of appearance, describing them as 'dripping in bling', that is, 'cheap, tasteless and usually gold-coloured jewellery' (Tweedie, 2004).

Moreover, chavs are portrayed as loud mouthed and aggressive. Male chavs in particular are often associated with violence and petty crime, such as football hooliganism, vandalism, assaults and muggings. This is captured by the notion that the term is an acronym for 'council housed and violent'. Chavs are also described as promiscuous and sexually irresponsible, and this is especially the case for 'chavettes', that is, female chavs, who are depicted as 'sluts' with no control over their sexuality. They are also associated with teenage pregnancy and motherhood. Thus, in a *Daily Mail* article entitled 'A-Z of chavs', one can read: 'PRAM: Any Chavette who isn't pushing one of these by the age of 14 is obviously frigid, infertile or a "lezza" [lesbian]' (Thomas, 2004). Moreover, chavs have often been portrayed as uneducated, lazy, unemployed welfare cheats lacking any willingness to work, who are happily using the welfare system paid for by 'us' hard-working respectable people. As the *Sun* put it:

> They just want to leech off the sweat of the rest of us …
> These freeloaders are not too thick to realise they can get
> more by scrounging on the dole rather than working.
> They've sussed that even with a minimum wage they can
> lie in their pits until the afternoon and still pick up a nice
> wedge, especially if they keep pushing out their soon-to-
> be-feral offspring. (Gaunt, 2008)

Thus, chavs have been constructed as non-respectable, white, working-class 'folk devils' who threaten the moral order of society through their sexual and reproductive activities, willing joblessness, antisocial behaviour and vulgar taste. Here a marginal class position, that is, a lack of economic and cultural capital, is tied to a 'dirty' and therefore racialised form of whiteness (see also Hall and Jefferson, 1975; Webster, 2008).

A contested public issue about class

An important aspect of the chav discourse is that it has made social class the subject of public discussion. This is significant, given the earlier silence around the topic in the British public sphere (Savage, 2000; Skeggs, 2004). Some cases of class contempt directed against chavs have become widely debated. One example is a YouTube video clip entitled 'Class Wars' made by pupils of Glenalmond College, one of Britain's foremost public schools. The video is a supposedly humorous take on a fox hunt, but one that involves the shooting of chavs instead of foxes. Another example is the media debate following the publication of a promotional e-mail sent by travel company Activities Abroad that offered 'chav free holidays'. It based this claim on the fact that names associated with chavs were absent from its database. The company's managing director, Alistair McLean, later defended the e-mail, stating:

"I simply feel it is time the middle-classes stood up for themselves. We make a positive contribution to our economy and watch it all be frittered away by people who simply can't be bothered ('bovvered'). /../ So regardless of whether it is class warfare or not I make no apology for proclaiming myself to be middle-class and a genuine contributor to our society." (Digitalspy, 2009)

In this statement, McLean contrasts respectable, hard-working middle-class people with chavs who threaten to destroy everything that the former built up. The huge volume of such strongly derogatory content directed against chavs in public discourse, not the least when articulated by journalists representing 'serious' news media, suggests that in many contexts, such language is legitimate.

Yet many commentators, especially from the Left, have criticised 'chav-bashing' as a form of classism or class-racism. This reflects the fact that in contemporary, fragmented public spheres, moral panics and other public issues are frequently contested (McRobbie and Thornton, 1995). One notable illustration of this was in 2008 when Tom Hampson, editor-in-chief of the *Fabian Review*, the journal published by the left-wing think-tank the Fabian Society, wrote an editorial that generated much debate. In this he argued that the term 'chav' should be banned, and that its usage 'is deeply offensive to a largely voiceless group and – especially when used in normal middle-class conversation or on national TV – it betrays a deep and revealing level of class hatred' (Hampson, 2008). This article was repeated in an opinion piece in the *Guardian* online (Hampson and Olchawski, 2008) and has been further explored in an influential book entitled *Chav: The Demonization of the Working Class* by writer and journalist Owen Jones (2011). The book created extensive debate and put issues of social class and the chav phenomenon further onto the public agenda, not only in Britain but also internationally.

Social control measures

In the wake of moral panics, measures of social control are typically instated in order to 'protect' the public from the threat posed by the 'folk devils' (Cohen, 2002 [1972]). This was also the case for the anxieties that surround chavs, who became the target of new and existing forms of policing. One such form of policing dealt with regulating access to public space. Shopping malls, pubs, night clubs and internet cafes started banning the wearing of garments or brands associated with chavs, including baseball caps, hoodies, tracksuits and clothes in Burberry check. One of the cases most covered by the media was the ban on 'hoodies' (hooded tops) in the Bluewater Shopping Centre in Kent in 2005 (see Hier et al, 2011).

Chavs have also been strongly associated with Anti-Social Behaviour Orders (ASBOs). First issued by the Labour government in 1997, but strengthened and broadened during 2003–04, an ASBO is a civil order serving 'to restrict the behaviour of a person likely to cause harm or distress to the public' (Oxford Dictionaries, nd). In common parlance, ASBO also refers to the kind of people against whom such civil orders are issued. Chavs are often conceived as ASBOs, as in the following definition of the term on Urban Dictionary (nd): '[ASBO is] an essential qualification for all chavs and general idiots who think that beating the shit out of random people walking down the street/ throwing bricks through people's windows/generally displaying how few brain cells they have, makes them look "hard"'. Chavs are often seen as glorifying ASBOS, and are supposed to believe that getting one is seen as a 'badge of honour'.

Conclusion: moralisation and the dialectics of class identity

In what way can the moralisation of chavs be considered a moral panic? The social reaction to chavs emerged suddenly and involved significant hostility. Thus, chavs were constructed as a folk devil threatening the moral and aesthetic order of British society. Chavs also became the targets of different forms of social control. However, contra fully fledged moral panics, there has been no discrete group of moral entrepreneurs organising campaigns against chavs in any systematic or extended fashion. Rather, the social reaction emerged and diffused spontaneously throughout the 'grassroots' of the public sphere. I would therefore argue that the chav phenomenon constitutes a sudden, strong form of social reaction with elements of a moral panic that is bound up with longer-term moralisation processes of white working-class people in Britain.

Through these moralisation processes the chav has been constructed as a non-respectable figure of the white British working class. This works dialectically: on the one hand, the chav becomes a stigmatising social identity in which certain white working-class people are positioned. On the other hand, these processes simultaneously enable middle-class and working-class people to position themselves as respectable and morally righteous. Notions of respectability have been central in constructing classed hierarchies of moral worth (Skeggs, 1997; Sayer, 2005). In Britain, this has entailed the long-standing moral denigration of certain groups of white working-class people as non-respectable (Stacey, 1960; Bott, 1964; Skeggs, 1997, 2004; Watt, 2006).

The emergence of the chav stereotype can be linked to the neoliberal economic restructuring and deindustrialisation of the last decades, which led to the rise of 'flexible' and poor work (McDowell, 2003), as well as to the increasing marginalisation, poverty and fragmentation of working-class communities, particularly in the North of England (see also Charlesworth, 2000; Turner, 2000). By the late 1990s, when New Labour came into power, there was no room for the marginalised white working-class in its vision of 21st-century Britain. As Haylett (2001) has shown, the political rhetoric of New Labour envisioned a multicultural, modern and progressive Britain in which white, poor working-class people simultaneously became cast as the unmodern, racist and backward 'other'. I would argue that the youth of this group has come to be further demonised and pathologised under the label 'chav'. It is also in this context of marginalised whiteness that the moralising discourse directed against chavs has become a widely legitimate form of class racism, which it would be impossible to direct against any ethnic or sexual minority with the same force (le Grand, 2013).

References

Bott, E. (1964) *Family and social network: Roles, norms and external relationships in ordinary urban families*, London: Tavistock Publications.

Bourdieu, P. (1984 [1979]) *Distinction: A social critique of the judgement of taste*, Cambridge, MA: Harvard University Press.

Bourdieu, P. (1986) 'The forms of capital', in J.G. Richardson (ed) *Handbook of theory and research for the sociology of education*, Westport, CT: Greenwood Press, pp 241–58.

Bourdieu, P. (1987) 'What makes a social class? On the theoretical and practical existence of groups', *Berkeley Journal of Sociology*, vol 22, pp 1–17.

Charlesworth, S.J. (2000) *A phenomenology of working-class experience*, Cambridge: Cambridge University Press.

Cohen, S. (2002 [1972]) *Folk devils and moral panics: The creation of the Mods and Rockers* (3rd edn), London: Routledge.

Critcher, C. (2009) 'Widening the focus: moral panics as moral regulation', *British Journal of Criminology*, vol 49, no 1, pp 17–34.

Critcher, C. (2013) 'New perspectives on anti-doping policy: from moral panic to moral regulation', *International Journal of Sport Policy and Politics*, vol 6, no 2, pp 153-69.

Dent, S. (2004) *Larpers and shroomers: The language report*, Oxford: Oxford University Press.

Digitalspy (2009) '"Chav-free" holidays offered by travel firm!!!', http://forums.digitalspy.co.uk/showthread.php?t=980152 (accessed 17 March 2015)

Gaunt, J. (2008) 'Karen's in a class of her own', *Sun* (18 April).

Hall, S. and Jefferson, T. (1975; 2nd edn 2006) *Resistance through Rituals, Youth Subcultures in Post-War Britain* (Cultural Studies Birmingham), London: Routledge.

Hampson, T. (2008) 'Drop the word "chav"', *Fabian Review*, vol 120, no 2, pp 19.

Hampson, T. and Olchawski, J. (2008) 'Ban the word "chav"', *Guardian* (15 July), www.theguardian.com/commentisfree/2008/jul/15/equality.language.

Haylett, C. (2001) 'Illegitimate subjects? Abject Whites, neoliberal modernisation, and middle-class multiculturalism', *Environment and Planning D: Society and Space*, vol 19, no 3, pp 351–70.

Hayward, K. and Yar, M. (2006) 'The "chav" phenomenon: consumption, media and the construction of a new underclass', *Crime, Media, Culture,* vol 2, no 1, pp 9–28.

Hier, S.P. (2002) 'Conceptualizing moral panic through a moral economy of harm', *Critical Sociology,* vol 28, no 3, pp 311–34.

Hier, S.P. (2008) 'Thinking beyond moral panic: risk, responsibility, and the politics of moralization', *Theoretical Criminology*, vol 12, no 2, pp 173–90.

Hier, S.P. (2011) 'Tightening the focus: moral panic, moral regulation and liberal government', *British Journal of Sociology,* vol 62, no 3, pp 523–41.

Hier, S.P., Lett, D., Walby, K. and Smith, A. (2011) 'Beyond folk devil resistance: linking moral panic and moral regulation', *Criminology and Criminal Justice*, vol 11, no 3, pp 259–76.

Hunt, A. (2011) 'Fractious rivals? Moral panics and moral regulation', in S.P. Hier (ed) *Moral panic and the politics of anxiety*, London: Routledge, pp 53–70.

Jones, O. (2011) *Chavs: The demonization of the working class*, London: Verso.

le Grand, E. (2010) *Class, place and identity in a satellite town*, Stockholm: Acta Universitatis Stockholmiensis.

le Grand, E. (2013) 'The "chav" as folk devil', in J. Petley, C. Critcher, J. Hughes and A. Rohloff (eds) *Moral panics in the contemporary world*, London: Bloomsbury, pp 215–34.

Lewis, J. (2004) 'In defence of snobbery', *Telegraph* (31 January).

McDowell, L. (2003) *Redundant masculinities? Employment change and white working class youth*, Oxford: Blackwell.

McRobbie, A. and Thornton, S. (1995) 'Rethinking "moral panic" for multi-mediated social worlds', *British Journal of Sociology*, vol 46, no 4, pp 559–74.

Oxford Dictionaries (nd) 'Asbo', www.oxforddictionaries.com/ definition/ english/ASBO (accessed 3 May 2013).

Savage, M. (2000) *Class analysis and social transformation*, Buckingham: Open University.

Sayer, A. (2005) *The moral significance of class*, Cambridge: Cambridge University Press.

Skeggs, B. (1997) *Formations of class and gender: Becoming respectable*, London: Sage.

Skeggs, B. (2004) *Class, self, culture*, London: Routledge.

Stacey, M. (1960) *Tradition and change: A study of Banbury*, Oxford: Oxford University Press.

Thomas, D. (2004) 'A-Z of chavs', *Daily Mail* (20 October).

Turner, R.L. (2000) *Coal was our life: An essay on life in a Yorkshire former pit town*, Sheffield: Sheffield Hallam University Press.

Tweedie, N. (2004) 'Cheltenham ladies and the chavs', *Telegraph* (14 December).

Urban Dictionary (nd) 'ASBO', ww.urbandictionary.com/define. php?term=ASBO (accessed 17 March 2015).

Watt, P. (2006) 'Respectability, roughness and "race": neighbourhood place images and the making of working-class social distinctions in London', *International Journal of Urban and Regional Research*, vol 30, no 4, pp 776–97.

Webster, C. (2008) 'Marginalized white ethnicity, race and crime', *Theoretical Criminology*, vol 12, no 3, pp 293–312.

FOUR

The presence of the absent parent: troubled families and the England 'riots' of 2011

Steve Kirkwood

Introduction

The 'riots' in England during August 2011 involved a level of public disturbance and destruction rarely seen in the United Kingdom. These events resulted in widespread speculation as to the causes of, and solutions to, the violence and looting. The public and media responses could be seen as constituting a 'moral panic' in relation to the people involved, particularly in terms of the scapegoating of the young people who took part in the 'riots'. In this regard, Prime Minister David Cameron argued that the involvement of many young people was related to poor parenting and absent fathers, and stated that he would seek to 'turn around the lives of the 120,000 most troubled families in the country'. This chapter explores the way in which 'troubled families' were portrayed as a cause of people's involvement in the 'riots' and critically examines the implications of such understandings of and responses to public unrest. In particular, it demonstrates how the discourse and related initiatives depoliticise 'riots'; how 'problem families' are portrayed as being a target for policy; and how the 'riots' were used to expand a policy direction already in place.

The 'riots'

On 4 August 2011, Mark Duggan, a 29-year-old black man from Tottenham, was shot dead by police. On 6 August, a group of approximately 200 people gathered at Tottenham police station seeking further information regarding the incident. There is evidence that police used aggressive tactics that provoked a reaction from the crowd (Reicher and Stott, 2011), which was followed by some members of the public setting police cars on fire, throwing various objects at the police and causing damage to certain commercial buildings. From 6 to 10 August, public disturbance spread to various parts of England and appeared to involve a variety of motivations, including protesting against discriminatory police practices, reacting to general inequalities in society and elements of opportunism (Reicher and Stott, 2011).

On 11 August 2011, Prime Minister David Cameron made a parliamentary speech on the events and the actions that were being taken to address them (Cameron, 2011a). He highlighted the death of Mark Duggan and the 'peaceful demonstrations' that initially followed, and asserted that these were 'then used as an excuse by opportunist thugs in gangs', leading to behaviour that constituted 'criminality pure and simple', thus illustrating Potter and Wetherell's (1987) idea that 'splitting' people into 'good' and 'bad' protestors is a way of condemning certain groups and behaviours while still appearing, on the surface, to be reasonable and understanding. In this case, people involved in the 'peaceful demonstrations' were portrayed as legitimate whereas those involved in other activities could be vilified as 'criminals', while avoiding dealing with the ways in which wider social issues and police relations might, in practice, structure both categories of behaviour.

Cameron also referred to the 'deeper problems' that provided the context for the 'riots':

> I have said before that there is a major problem in our society with children growing up not knowing the difference between right and wrong. This is not about poverty, it's about culture. A culture that glorifies violence, shows disrespect to authority, and says everything about rights but nothing about responsibilities. In too many cases, the parents of these children – if they are still around

> – don't care where their children are or who they are
> with, let alone what they are doing. (Cameron, 2011a)

Here the problem was portrayed as lying with young people – 'children' – and the way in which they had been raised. Importantly, the 'riots' were presented as immoral behaviour perpetrated by those who did not know any better and were thereby depoliticised. Furthermore, the inequalities in society – and the government's role in maintaining or exacerbating these inequalities – were dismissed, thus reinforcing an image of the riots as non-political. Rather, the 'problems' were presented as relating to 'culture' and the ways that this might facilitate or endorse 'rioting' behaviours. If Cameron's account functioned to provide a broader 'context' or source of the riots, rather than pointing to structural issues or problems of inequality, it thus shifted blame onto the parents and families of the 'rioters'.

'Troubled families'

On 15 August, David Cameron gave a more extended account regarding the 'riots'. He discounted explanations relating to 'race', 'government cuts' or 'poverty' and stated:

> No, this was about behaviour ...
>   ... people showing indifference to right and wrong ...
>   ... people with a twisted moral code ...
>   ... people with a complete absence of self-restraint.
> (Cameron, 2011b)

As with the accounts provided in his previous speech, here he explicitly rejected explanations for the 'riots' that focused on the actions of the government or on inequality. This depoliticised the 'riots' and suggested solutions that focused on individual rather than structural issues. He specifically emphasised the role of families and parents:

Let me start with families. The question people asked over and over again last week was 'where are the parents? Why aren't they keeping the rioting kids indoors?' Tragically that's been followed in some cases by judges rightly lamenting: 'why don't the parents even turn up when their children are in court?' Well, join the dots and you have a clear idea about why some of these young people were behaving so terribly. Either there was no one at home, they didn't much care or they'd lost control.

Families matter. I don't doubt that many of the rioters out last week have no father at home. Perhaps they come from one of the neighbourhoods where it's standard for children to have a mum and not a dad ... where it's normal for young men to grow up without a male role model, looking to the streets for their father figures, filled up with rage and anger. So if we want to have any hope of mending our broken society, family and parenting is where we've got to start. (Cameron, 2011b)

Here the parents are condemned for not taking enough interest in their children, specifically for being absent, uncaring or incompetent. The implication is that 'rioting' behaviour was a result of parents who were not present, not interested or not capable of raising their children appropriately. More specifically, the account condemns fathers for their absence and asserts a causal link between a father's absence and children's violent behaviour.

A key element of Cameron's stated approach related to the notion of 'troubled families':

And we need more urgent action, too, on the families that some people call 'problem', others call 'troubled'. The ones that everyone in their neighbourhood knows and often avoids. [...] Now that the riots have happened I will make sure that we clear away the red tape and the bureaucratic wrangling, and put rocket boosters under

> this programme ... with a clear ambition that within the lifetime of this Parliament we will turn around the lives of the 120,000 most troubled families in the country. (Cameron, 2011b)

An important aspect of Cameron's description of these families is the use of the terms 'problem' and 'troubled'. More specifically, labelling them as 'problem families' suggests that they are the source of the problem and that they constitute a problem for other people. In contrast, 'troubled families' implies that they face troubles and that they are the ones having to deal with difficulties that affect them from external sources. Although he uses the term 'troubled families' later in the extract, the way in which he introduces these two labels suggests at least an ambivalence towards the families and the ways of conceiving of them. The idea that they may be 'problem families' more than 'troubled families' is reinforced by his suggestion that they are '[t]he ones that everyone in their neighbourhood knows and often avoids'. Cameron clarified his use of the phrase in a subsequent speech:

> Officialdom might call them 'families with multiple disadvantages'. Some in the press might call them 'neighbours from hell'. Whatever you call them, we've known for years that a relatively small number of families are the source of a large proportion of the problems in society. (Cameron, 2011c)

The account suggests that Cameron's view is that these families are the cause of the problems rather than merely those who are on the receiving end of such problems (that is, 'problem families' more than 'troubled families').

As Cameron makes clear, his approach towards these 'troubled families' had begun several months before the riots occurred. A key part of Cameron's approach is the goal to 'turn around the lives of the 120,000 most troubled families in the country'. This aim had resulted in the development of the Troubled Families Unit within the government to oversee the work on this matter. One of the interesting issues relates to the '120,000' families identified in Cameron's speech. The Department for Communities (nd) released a document explaining the origins of this figure. Levitas (2012) challenged the figure, including the £9 billion the government suggested these families cost the taxpayer, due to their 'troubles'. An important aspect of Levitas' critique is that the estimate is based on a figure from a study that found that 2% of the study sample met at least five of the following seven criteria, and were therefore multiply disadvantaged:

> No parent in the family is in work;
> Family lives in overcrowded housing;
> No parent has any qualifications;
> Mother has mental health problems;
> At least one parent has a long-standing limiting illness, disability or infirmity;
> Family has low income (below 60% of median income);
> Family cannot afford a number of food and clothing items. (Levitas, 2012)

It is clear that these criteria relate to issues of unemployment, poverty, illness and disability. This is very different from the issues of absent parents, violence, criminality, gang involvement, poor parenting and lack of morals identified by Cameron in his speeches. As Levitas (2012, p 10) points out, the government's account of these families constitutes an instance of 'slippage from the criteria of multiple deprivation to those of anti-social behaviour'. Far from a mere error of transposition, this shift is evident in Cameron's (2011c) speech, where he suggests that there is no substantial difference between 'families with multiple disadvantages' and 'neighbours from hell'. To the contrary, these different criteria could mark the difference between families that *face* trouble and families that *make* trouble. Of course, the ambiguity inherent in the notion 'troubled families' allows for such slippage, while introducing a negative moral evaluation of families that experience a variety of problems.

Moral panic?

I will now explore whether this issue can be understood from the perspective of the concept of 'moral panic' (Cohen, 1972), drawing on Goode and Ben-Yehuda's (2009) model. This argues that the following characteristics are likely to be in place for a moral panic to ensue: concern, hostility, consensus, disproportion and volatility. There is clear evidence that the 'riots', as discussed already and as demonstrated by Hedge and MacKenzie (2012), resulted in widespread concern and hostility. I will therefore focus on the remaining criteria.

Consensus

Reicher and Stott (2011) claim that: 'Within a week of the riots there was a clear consensus that the riots were all about criminality [...] Within a month, that consensus had crystallized into policy.'

But how far was there 'a clear consensus'? In an earlier publication, Reicher and Hopkins (2001) suggest that the greater the consensus in terms of the significance of an event in a nation's history, the more potential disagreement over its meaning. In the case of the riots, Ed Miliband (2011), Leader of the Opposition, explicitly rejected David Cameron's account and argued that the types of values reflected in the actions of 'looters' were modelled through the 'greedy, selfish and immoral' behaviour of elite sections of society, including bankers, MPs and journalists. Furthermore, a public survey by eDigitalResearch (nd) found various levels of support for different explanations, including greed and lack of respect, poor parenting, police tactics and lack of opportunities for young people. Importantly, Newburn et al (2011) argue that many of the 'rioters' characterised their own behaviour as 'protesting', thus challenging other accepted accounts. All of this suggests that consensus was not just absent, but an impossibility. Rather than establishing consensus, I believe that it may be more helpful to consider the extent to which elites are able to produce legitimacy in relation to a social issue.

Disproportion

Turning to the question of the proportionality of the response, the cost of damage from the 'riots' was estimated at over £500 million (Riots, Communities and Victims Panel, 2012). David Cameron (2011c) suggested that the '120,000 troubled families' cost the taxpayer approximately £9 billion a year, and allocated £448 million to address the situation. Sentences for those convicted of crimes during the riots were criticised by some commentators as being too harsh, although others suggested they were appropriate (BBC, 2011). Although it is possible to compare damage costs to the cost of 'solutions' or to compare sentences for similar crimes, this will not resolve the issue of proportionality, as the extent and nature of the problem, and the appropriate response, are exactly the issues under dispute. Defining a response as 'proportionate' as opposed to 'disproportionate' must, I would argue, be understood as a rhetorical accomplishment in itself.

Volatility

How far can the riots be considered, in moral panic parlance, to have been volatile? They did 'erupt fairly suddenly' (Goode and Ben-Yehuda, 2009, p 41), but how far were they a unique, identifiable phenomenon in their own right? Hier et al (2011, p 260) argue that 'moral panics represent episodes of contestation and negotiation that emerge from and contribute to or reinforce broader processes of moral regulation'. In this regard, both main political parties have focused on the responsibilisation of parents, with Labour's Family Intervention Projects for the '50,000 most chaotic families' (Gregg, 2010), followed up by David Cameron's commitment to address the '120,000 most troubled families'. This would suggest that the response to the 'riots' constituted a continuation and emphasis of the attention on such families, rather than merely a 'knee jerk' reaction to the 2011 'riots'.

Discussion

The way the 'riots' were portrayed and linked to 'troubled families' functions to depoliticise the 'riots' and shifts attention away from structural causes, while 'slippage' between families that *face* problems and families that *cause* problems leads to stigmatisation. Whether they provide an example of the unfolding of a classic moral panic, as characterised by Goode and Ben-Yehuda (2009), seems doubtful. It has been demonstrated that consensus was not only unlikely, but an impossibility. Similarly, proportionality is exactly the issue at stake and there are no 'objective' criteria to resolve the dispute. Following Hier et al (2011), although the 'riots' themselves appeared to be an indication of volatility, the governmental response regarding a focus on responsibility, out-of-control youth and poor parenting constituted relative continuity in policy. This analysis thus illustrates the way in which a significant event can be used to bring attention and resources to an issue and policy strategy that is already in place, despite tenuous causal links.

As highlighted by Pearce and Charman (2011), research on moral panics has involved a range of theoretical perspectives, including Cohen's (1972) focus on labelling, Hall et al's (1978) Marxist influences and Goode and Ben-Yehuda's (2011) social constructionist approach. The present discussion suggests that a discursive approach (Potter and Wetherell, 1987), which focuses on the way that language functions to actively construct social realities, may be helpful in understanding certain aspects of events that could be deemed 'moral panics'. Such an approach should help to extend the scope of such research while potentially addressing some of the common criticisms of the ways in which moral panics are conceived. In relation to Goode and Ben-Yehuda's criteria, such an approach could examine: how concern is manifested and justified; the nature of the hostility; the way people legitimise their responses and claim consensus; how responses are portrayed as being proportionate or disproportionate; and how the apparent volatile nature of the response may be understood within a context of relative continuity in terms of the discursive construction of 'folk devils' and related policy responses.

Conclusions

The England 'riots' of 2011 illustrate an instance where the UK government mobilised a policy for intervening with 'troubled families', based on tenuous connections between the targets of the intervention and the original 'riots'. Furthermore, it is helpful to understand this situation in the context of continuity – in the sense of a policy direction that was already underway – rather than merely as a reactive response to extreme events. When analysing the situation, it is useful to see how the situation and appropriate responses were discursively constructed by key players in the government, as well as by alternative voices. This approach highlights that 'slippage' in language ('troubled families' versus 'problem families'), the construction of consensus and arguments over proportionality function to legitimise or criticise policy responses. The concept of 'moral panics' helps to understand extreme events such as 'riots'; however, some of the key criteria for a 'moral panic' are exactly the things that are most contested in this context and 'objective' measures will remain elusive. For this reason, it is important to go beyond the moral-panic heuristic (Rohloff and Wright 2010), drawing on alternative ideas such as those from discourse analysis, in order to strengthen our understanding.

References

BBC (2011) 'Some England riot sentences "too severe"', www.bbc.co.uk/news/uk-14553330 (17 August).

Cameron, D. (2011a) 'PM's speech on Big Society', www.gov.uk/government/speeches/pms-speech-on-big-society (accessed 17 March 2015).

Cameron, D. (2011b) 'PM's speech on the fightback after the riots', www.gov.uk/government/speeches/pms-speech-on-the-fightback-after-the-riots (accessed 17 March 2015).

Cameron, D. (2011c) 'Troubled families speech', www.gov.uk/government/speeches/troubled-families-speech (accessed 17 March 2015).

Cohen, S. (1972) *Folk devils and moral panics*, London: MacGibbon & Kee.

Department for Communities (nd) Troubled family estimates explanatory note, http://webarchive.nationalarchives.gov. uk/20120919132719/www.communities.gov.uk/documents/ newsroom/pdf/2053538.pdf (accessed 17 March 2015)

eDigitalResearch (nd) *England riots survey – August 2011: Summary of findings*, https://www.edigitalresearch.com/files/sky/news_panel/ riot_survey_summary_of_findings.pdf.

Goode, E. and Ben-Yehuda, N. (2009) *Moral panics: The social construction of deviance* (2nd edn), Chichester, UK: Wiley-Blackwell.

Gregg, D. (2010) *Family Intervention Projects: A classic case of policy-based evidence*, www.crimeandjustice.org.uk/sites/crimeandjustice.org.uk/ files/family%20intervention.pdf (accessed 17 March 2015).

Hall, S., Critcher, C., Jefferson, T., Clarke, J. and Roberts, B. (1978) *Policing the crisis: Mugging, the state, and law and order*, London: Macmillan.

Hedge, N. and MacKenzie, A. (2012) 'Riots and reactions: Hypocrisy and disaffiliation?', Philosophy of Education Society of Great Britain Annual Conference, New College, Oxford, 30 March–1 April, www. yumpu.com/en/document/view/25297348/riots-and-reactions-hypocrisy-and-disaffiliation-philosophy-of-
(accessed 17 March 2015)

Hier, S.P., Lett, D., Walby, K. and Smith, A. (2011) 'Beyond folk devil resistance: Linking moral panic and moral regulation', *Criminology and Criminal Justice*, vol 11, pp 259–76.

Levitas, R. (2012) 'There may be "trouble" ahead: What we know about those 120,000 "troubled" families', www.poverty.ac.uk/ sites/poverty/files/WP%20Policy%20Response%20No.3-%20 %20%27Trouble%27%20ahead%20%28Levitas%20Final%20 21April2012%29.pdf.

Miliband, E. (2011) 'Full transcript – speech on the riots', *New Statesman*, www.newstatesman.com/politics/2011/08/society-young-heard-riots.

Newburn, T., Lewis, P., Addley, E. and Taylor, M. (2011) 'David Cameron, the Queen and the rioters' sense of injustice', in D. Roberts (ed), *Reading the riots: Investigating England's summer of disorder*, London: Guardian Books. [Kindle Edition]

Pearce, J.M. and Charman, E. (2011) 'A social psychological approach to understanding moral panic', *Crime, Media, Culture*, vol 7, pp 293–311.

Potter, J. and Wetherell, M. (1987) *Discourse and social psychology: Beyond attitudes and behaviour*, London: Sage.

Reicher, S. and Hopkins, N. (2001) *Self and nation*, London: Sage.

Reicher, S. and Stott, C. (2011) *Mad mobs and Englishmen? Myths and realities of the 2011 riots*, London: Constable & Robinson Ltd.

Riots, Communities and Victims Panel (2012) *After the riots: The final report of the Riots Communities and Victims Panel*, http://riotspanel. independent.gov.uk/wp-content/uploads/2012/03/Riots-Panel-Final-Report1.pdf.

Rohloff, A. and Wright, S. (2010) 'Moral panic and social theory: beyond the heuristic', *Current Sociology*, vol 58, no 3, pp 403–19.

FIVE

Patient safety: a moral panic

William James Fear

Introduction

This chapter introduces a new subject into the moral panic literature – patient safety – and in doing so explores the ways in which moral panics around patient safety have been used by physicians as part of a deliberate strategy in order to bring about institutional transformation. It is important to note that the term 'moral panic' has a much longer lineage than is commonly thought to be the case. It first appeared in the *Quarterly Christian Spectator* in 1830, and then again in *The Journal of Health Conducted by an Association of Physicians* in 1831. In this journal, a French physician visiting Sunderland (in England) praised the English government for its approach to the cholera epidemic. He congratulated the government for not surrounding the town with a cordon of troops which as 'a physical preventive would have been ineffectual and would have produced a moral panic far more fatal than the disease now is' (unknown, 1831, p 180). The term was picked up much later, in 1964, with the Canadian sociologist Marshall McLuhan's ground-breaking work on the influence of the media, and later expanded by Jock Young (1971) and Stan Cohen (1972). Given the historical nature of the phenomenon, it seems both unrealistic and unlikely to assume that moral panics are inherently media driven. However, it seems equally realistic and likely to assume that the media plays, at times, a key role, as we will see in the case-study examples that follow.

The chapter focuses on two case-study examples, anaesthesia as a specific medical intervention and healthcare more broadly, noting that there are many more possible cases of which 'injury to the person' is a subfield that could have been considered, including, for example, automotive safety, consumer-product safety and medical insurance.

Moral panic and institutionalism

A moral panic may be described simply as a perceived threat to society and its cultural values, based on a hitherto unacknowledged or taboo subject. There may be a perceived individual, group or class of individual who is held to be responsible for the threat, usually portrayed in the media as 'folk devils'; those who identify the threat are often known as 'moral entrepreneurs' (Cohen, 1972). However, as the historical examples demonstrate, there is no reason to assume that a moral panic requires either folk devils or moral entrepreneurs. Instead, what we saw in the *Journal of Health Conducted by an Association of Physicians* reference was the early seeds of institutional, if not moral, entrepreneurship in relation to epidemics, and the strong inclination on the part of physicians to wrest control of perceived and potential epidemics from government and policy makers.

Patient safety provides, in my view, an illustration of a phenomenon where there is evidently moral entrepreneurship, but no clear folk devils. Moral entrepreneurship is exercised as a means to build an institution within healthcare. Simply put, the moral entrepreneur identifies a quantifiable number of deaths associated with a practice (for example, anaesthesia) or the practice of medicine (for example, hospital care). These deaths are then calculated as far in excess of what could, and should, be reasonably expected; the problem is not any one individual or group but, rather, the very nature of the practice itself. Following this, an argument is made that there is a resource requirement needed to address this problem, and the problem is couched in terms of an epidemic. Comparisons are made to other areas of practice, or other epidemics, where unnecessary deaths have been reduced ('saved lives') following the provision of resources. The saving of lives (sometimes phrased as the reduction of injury to the person) is mooted as a measurable and identifiable outcome, should the necessary and sufficient resources be made available. Not only that, the saving of lives is couched as a moral imperative – a necessary response to the dire state of affairs now made known.

We turn now to the two case-study examples: anaesthesia and healthcare. An important distinction must be made at the outset. In the case of anaesthesia, I will argue that a moral panic was suppressed and contained within the medical community; as a result, it did not lead to any substantive acquisition and redistribution of resources, and the only outcome was that insurance premiums were reduced. In contrast, in the case of healthcare, attempts at suppression were overcome and a moral panic ensued, and continues to ensue, on a global scale. This has led to substantive acquisition and redistribution of resources, but no measurable outcome as yet.

Patient safety in anaesthesia

Anaesthesia provides one of the clearest examples of moral entrepreneurship that was contained within a community. As early as 1954, Beecher and Todd published a paper in the *Annals of Surgery* that deplored the number of deaths occurring in anaesthesia, comparing it to an epidemic and arguing for further resources. They wrote:

> Anaesthesia might be likened to a disease which afflicts 8,000,000 persons in the United States each year. More than twice as many citizens out of the total population of the country die from anaesthesia as die from poliomyelitis. Deaths from anaesthesia are certainly a matter for 'public health' concern. When one thinks of the millions of dollars rightly spent each year on research to combat poliomyelitis and the next-to-nothing, comparatively, spent in research to overcome the hazards of anaesthesia, a very great need is evident. (Beecher and Todd, 1954, p 28)

Other medics disagreed; an article in the same journal the following year by Abajtan, Arrowood, Barret et al (1955) took issue with Beecher and Todd's claims, and since then the subject has been regularly revisited within the profession. Over time, the problem of avoidable harm was recognised within anaesthesia, resulting in the establishment in the US of the Anesthesia Patient Safety Foundation (APSF, nd) in late 1985. The APSF describes itself on its website as an 'independent, non-profit corporation with representation from anesthesiologists, nurse anesthetists, nurses, manufacturers of equipment and drugs, regulators, risk managers, attorneys, insurers and engineers'; its vision is that 'no patient shall be harmed by anesthesia' (APSF, nd). Meanwhile, the UK's Safe Anaesthesia Liaison Group is also firmly institutionalised within the remit of the Royal College of Anaesthetists of Great Britain and Ireland. The scale of preventable harm and related deaths from anaesthesia remains disputed and disputable today. This can, in summary, be seen as a panic that never really took off; patient safety in relation to anaesthesia remains located firmly within the boundaries of the medical profession. We will see a very different picture in relation to the moral panic around healthcare.

Patient safety in healthcare

The origins of the concept of 'patient safety' in healthcare are often erroneously assumed to lie with the publication of the Institute of Medicine's report *To Err is Human* (Kohn, Corrigan and Donaldson, 1999). In fact, this concept can be traced back to a publication by Schimmel (1964) on the problems of preventable harm in hospitalised care. This work was later extended to include medical malpractice litigation in the *Harvard Studies* (Brennan, Leape, Laird et al, 1991; Leape, Brennan, Laird et al, 1991). From here on, moral entrepreneurship was exercised within the physician community, to much criticism from within the community. The matter was resolved in 1994/95 with a paradigm shift within the community. However, the moral entrepreneurship continued and the report *To Err is Human* is effectively a rewrite of *Human Error in Medicine* (Bogner, 1994). It is suggested that it is no accident that the writing of *To Err is Human* was undertaken by a journalist and the report was 'leaked' to the press the day before its official publication.

The basis of the claim made in *To Err is Human* is: 'at least 44,000 Americans die each year as a result of medical errors. The results of the New York study suggest the number may be as high as 98,000 ... deaths due to medical errors exceed the number attributable to the 8th-leading cause of death. More people die in a given year as a result of medical errors than from motor vehicle accidents (43,458), breast cancer (42,297), or AIDS' (Kohn et al, 1999, p 1). The report went on to argue for substantial resources to address this concern and it subsequently successfully attracted a substantial level of resource. More importantly, the report marked a global shift in policy and legislation in healthcare as governments and related organisations rushed to address this seeming problem. For example, the World Health Organization (WHO) launched the World Alliance for Patient Safety (2004) in response to a World Health Assembly Resolution (2002) that urges member states to pay the closest possible attention to the problem of patient safety. In 2005, the European Commission published the Luxemburg Declaration on Patient Safety and there has been legislation such as the US Patient Safety and Quality Improvement Act of 2005 and the Danish Patient Safety Act 2003. Throughout this, there has been a strong 'recognition' of the 'need' for a body of research to inform practice and procedures, and a 'need' for centralised, blame-free error-reporting mechanisms (see, for example, Jensen, 2008; Fischbacher-Smith and Fischbacher-Smith, 2009; and Waring, Rowley, Dingwall et al, 2010). Since the early 2000s national patient safety monitoring organisations have been created in many countries, for example, in the US (the National Center for Patient Safety and the National Patient Safety Foundation), the UK (the National Patient Safety Agency and the National Reporting and Learning Service), Australia (the Australian Patient Safety Foundation), Denmark, Canada, Spain, Sweden and Switzerland, in the form of both public bodies and charitable organisations. In the UK, quality is held to be the prime focus of the NHS and patient safety is the 'first dimension' within this; senior management have quality and patient safety as key responsibilities (Department of Health, 2000; House of Commons Health Committee, 2009; National Patient Safety Agency, 2009).

So far, so good. Who could possibly disagree with a focus on patient safety? Examining this more closely, we find that some of the principal actors in this process of institution building openly recognise that the new concern for patient safety has not led to improvements in either safety or quality of care (for example, Leape, Berwick, Clancy et al, 2009; Jha, Prasopa-Plaizier, Larizgoitia et al, 2010; Woodward, Mytton, Lemer et al., 2010). To be clear, specific changes in practice for identified interventions have led to improvements for that practice in that intervention in the hospitals where the change in protocol has been correctly implemented. But a recent report (*Making Health Care Safer II*, Agency for Healthcare Research and Quality, 2013), noted that of 100 patient safety interventions reviewed, only 10 had sufficient evidence of effectiveness and implementation to be 'strongly encouraged' for adoption. Indeed, we can equally argue that if the quality of healthcare in the UK post-1999 is anything to go by, then a logical conclusion from the same arguments operationalised by the moral entrepreneurs is that patient safety initiatives have increased preventable harm in healthcare, not reduced it, by encouraging attention and resources to be focused too narrowly on specific targets. And of course, this also depends largely on whether or not we can purport to have an accurate and unbiased measure of preventable harm or an equally unbiased and accurate proxy. In sum, the foundations of patient safety in healthcare rest firmly on a moral panic that has little resemblance to the problem identified by Schimmel (1964). The act of moral entrepreneurship was extended beyond the bounds of the professional community and into the wider public domain. Once this happened, a full-blown moral panic ensued and continues to this day.

Discussion

Patient safety is a global institution and a global industry (Fear and Azambuja, 2014); this should come as no surprise when we consider the broader and deeper history of medicine and healthcare (Starr, 1982). The profession has developed and honed its institution-building capabilities over centuries, and this is but one readily identifiable demonstration of this.

The use of moral panic as a means to facilitate institution building in healthcare calls into question some of our existing understandings of moral panic in a number of key ways. Firstly, it challenges any notion that moral panics are always driven by the media; what we see instead is the media picking up and publicising a cause célèbre already articulated by the medical community (the moral entrepreneurs, in moral panic parlance). Secondly, there were no 'folk devils' in either of the case-study examples discussed here. There was, however, a clear 'episode' within healthcare that was couched in terms of an epidemic, which physicians have tried to institutionalise as their domain of policy at various times since at least 1830, and, in their doing so, the end result has been sizeable political and social change, just as moral panic theory (for example, Cohen, 1972) suggests. There is little evidence that 'moral crusaders', as outlined by Hall, Critcher, Jefferson et al (1978), joined forces in the process. Rather, physicians engaged directly in control of the entrepreneurial process. The contention that 'moral entrepreneurs launch crusades, which occasionally turn into panics, to make sure that certain rules take hold and are enforced' (Goode and Ben-Yehuda, 2009, p 67) is thus clearly supported. Of course, moral panic is not the only way of conceptualising this story; patient safety could also be seen as illustrative of a crisis in risk society (Ungar, 2001). However, given the historic reference to moral panic in the early medical journal in 1831, I believe that there is good reason to continue to frame this as a moral panic. Perhaps most importantly of all for our discussion, patient safety demonstrates that a moral panic can itself be an object, not merely a societal response to an external threat. Moral entrepreneurs use moral panics as tools to bring about institutional change; their use of 'evidence-informed' argument and publication in 'scientific' journals only adds weight to their claims. Put another way, publication in a leading scientific journal does not preclude the operationalisation of a moral panic – this is a caution to all of us (academics, researchers and policy makers) who engage in claims making.

Conclusion

There is no question that the moral panic of 'patient safety' has had an enormous impact on policy and practice, including in the form of legislation in most 'Western democracies'. There are lessons here about the way in which moral panics are taken account of; we need to go beyond explanations that locate causes with the media and folk devils. Beyond this, I have argued that professional and other collectives make use of a moral panic as a means for acquiring resources. This can take place over substantial periods of time and may result in institution building. The moral panics presented here led to substantial global institutions being built and the transformation of existing institutions; this had further impact on resource distribution. While there has been post-hoc justification of the process, there has also been some acknowledgement that the process did not always result in improvements 'on the ground'. We might conclude, therefore, that while a moral panic may result in resource distribution, this may not necessarily lead to the desired improvements.

References

Abajtan Jr, J., Arrowood, J., Barret, G., Dwyer, R.H., Eversole, C.S., Fine, U.H., Hand, J.H. and Woodbridge, L.V. (1955) 'Critique of "A Study of the Deaths Associated with Anaesthesia and Surgery"', *Annals of Surgery*, vol 142, no 1, pp 138–41.

Agency for Healthcare Research and Quality (2013) *Making Health Care Safer II: An Updated Critical Analysis of the Evidence for Patient Safety Practices*, Evidence Reports/Technology Assessments, no 211, Report no: 13-E001-EF, Rockville, MD: Agency for Healthcare Research and Quality (US), www.ncbi.nlm.nih.gov/books/NBK133363/ (accessed April 2014).

APSF (nd) About APSF, www.apsf.org/about_history.php.

Beecher, H.K. and Todd, D.P. (1954) 'A Study of the Deaths Associated with Anaesthesia and Surgery', *Annals of Surgery*, vol 140, no 1, pp 2–34.

Bogner, S. (ed) (1994) *Human error in medicine*, Hillsdale, NJ: Lawrence Erlbaum Associates.

Brennan, T A., Leape, L.L., Laird, N.M. et al (1991) 'Incidence of adverse events and negligence in hospitalized patients: Results of the Harvard Medical Practice Study I', *New England Journal of Medicine*, vol 324, pp 370–6.

Cohen, S. (1972) *Folk devils and moral panics: The creation of the Mods and the Rockers,* London: MacGibbon and Kee.

Department of Health (2000) *An organisation with a memory*, Norwich: The Stationery Office.

Fear, W.J. and Azambuja, R. (2014) 'Narrative and deliberative instauration: The use of narrative as process and artefact in the social construction of institutions', *Learning, Culture and Social Interaction*, online publication complete: 14 May, doi: 10.1016/j.lcsi.2014.04.002.

Fischbacher-Smith, D. and Fischbacher-Smith, M. (2009) 'We may remember but what did we learn? Dealing with errors, crimes and misdemeanours around adverse events in healthcare', *Financial Accounting and Management*, vol 25, no 4, pp 451–74.

Goode, E. and Ben-Yehuda, N. 2009 (1994) *Moral panics: The social construction of deviance*, 2nd edn, Malden: Wiley-Blackwell.

Hall, S., Critcher, C., Jefferson, T., Clarke, J. and Roberts, B. (1978) *Policing the crisis: Mugging, the state, and law and order*, Critical Social Studies, London: Macmillan.

House of Commons Health Committee (2009) *Patient safety*, London: The Stationery Office.

Jensen, C.B. (2008) 'Sociology, systems and (patient) safety: Knowledge translations in healthcare policy', *Society, Health and Illness*, vol 30, no 2, pp 309–24.

Jha, A.K., Prasopa-Plaizier, N., Larizgoitia, I. and Bates, D.W. (2010) 'Patient safety research: an overview of the global evidence', *Quality and Safety in Health Care*, vol 19, no 1, pp 42–7.

Kohn, L.T., Corrigan, J.M. and Donaldson, M.S. (eds) (1999/2000) *To Err is Human: Building a Safer Health System*, Committee on Quality of Health Care in America, Institute of Medicine, Washington, DC: National Academy Press, www.nap.edu/catalog.php?record_id=9728 (accessed May 2010).

Leape, L.L., Berwick, D., Clancy, C. et al (2009) 'Transforming healthcare: a safety imperative', *Quality of Safety and Healthcare*, vol 18, pp 424–42.

Leape, L.L., Brennan, T.A., Laird, N.M. et al (1991) 'The nature of adverse events in hospitalized patients: Results of the Harvard Medical Practice Study II', *New England Journal of Medicine*, vol 324, no 6, pp 377–84.

McLuhan, M. (1964) *Understanding media: The extensions of man*, New York: Signet.

National Patient Safety Agency (2009) *Seven steps to patient safety in general practice*, London: National Patient Safety Agency.

Schimmel, E.M. (1964) 'The hazards of hospitalization', *Quality and Safety in Healthcare*, vol 12, pp 58–64 (repr 2003).

Starr, P. (1982) *The social transformation of American medicine: The rise of a sovereign profession and the making of a vast industry*, New York: Basic Books.

Unknown (1831) 'Safeguards against the cholera', *The Journal of Health*, vol 3, no 2, 179–83, https://archive.org/stream/journalofhealth03slsn/journalofhealth03slsn_djvu.txt (accessed 17 March 2015).

Ungar, S. (2001) 'Moral panic versus the risk society: the implications of the changing sites of social anxiety', *British Journal of Sociology*, vol 52, no 2, pp 271–91.

Waring, J., Rowley, E., Dingwall, R., Palmer, C. and Murcott, T. (2010) 'Narrative review of the UK Patient Safety Research Portfolio', *Journal of Health Services Research Policy*, vol 15, no 1, pp 26–32.

Woodward, H.I., Mytton, O.T., Lemer, C. et al (2010) 'What have we learned about interventions to reduce medical errors?' *Annual Review of Public Health*, vol 31, no 1, pp 479–97.

Young, J. (1971) *The drugtakers: The social meaning of drug use*, London: Judson, McGibbon and Kee.

Afterword

Neil Hume

I remember first coming across Cohen's ground-breaking work on moral panics when I was an undergraduate sociology student; featuring evocative accounts of leather-clad rockers clashing with sharp-suited soul aficionados on the beaches of Brighton, Cohen analysed the process by which certain groups came to be deemed as threats to the social order by the media and establishment figures, and how public attitudes were manipulated to generate a groundswell of intolerance. It was irresistible stuff for the younger, left-lurching, Che Guevara-worshipping incarnation of myself. Yet, during my post-graduate training to become a social worker, and the several years I have spent working in the criminal justice system and children's services, it is not a body of work that I have ever returned to. When I read the contributions in this volume, which focus on the complex relationship between moral panics, the state and the profession of social work, I realise how many of the ideas and issues presented here speak to my day-to-day experience of being a front-line practitioner.

As the Introduction to this byte acknowledges, the concept of the state is somewhat nebulous and notoriously difficult to nail down. Unsurprisingly, many different sociologists have wrestled with the subject. One of the most influential was Weber (1994 [1919]), who sought to explain how the nature of the state has evolved throughout history. He suggested that the success of early forms of social organisation hinged on the charismatic influence of certain leaders. Feudal monarchies would later invoke the power of tradition and custom to maintain their subjects' loyalty. In liberal democracies the state commandeers the technical expertise required to operate a complex system of laws, regulations and public institutions, but also monopolises the legal use of any violent force. The key contribution of Hall et al (1978) was to recognise how the state could suppress political challenges to its authority in more subtle ways: through exploiting public concerns about certain social issues, such as crime, the state can justify the introduction of policies that effectively erode civil liberties. As many social workers involved in some form of safeguarding role in relation to children and adults are employees of the state, I felt that Hall's theories posed some unsettling questions for our profession, which I explore below.

In Kirkwood's Chapter Four, on the riots that took place in North London over the summer of 2011, he draws on the idea of moral panic to suggest that the government pushed a particular perspective on the situation that portrayed the participants as the products of poor parenting (and feckless fathers); and in its so doing the complex economic and social factors that contributed to this explosive expression of collective disaffection were side-lined within the public discourse. Moreover, to question this official – but highly politicised – account of what caused this disturbance was, in the eyes of the various claims makers and moral entrepreneurs, tantamount to approving arson. In a similar fashion, McKendrick (Chapter Two) describes how certain politicians sought to connect public concerns around the radicalisation of young Muslim men in the wake of the unprovoked murder of an off-duty soldier to the government's social policy initiative of providing intensive support to families that it deemed were in (or a source of) trouble. Thus, a flagship welfare programme designed, ostensibly, to help the most vulnerable children in society was explicitly linked to a raft of anti-terrorist initiatives, and the complex reasons why specific young people might come to identify with particular extremist organisations became conflated with a moral claim that there was a need to tackle dysfunctional families across society. So the contradictory messages that the state is sending to many families – that they are entitled to support from social work to overcome their difficulties but that they are also regarded as the source of many social problems, including future civil disobedience and potential terrorist acts – is likely to make them far less inclined to engage with state agencies, which in turn could make them more vulnerable. As practitioners we recognise that families either choose or are compelled to engage with social workers for a whole variety of reasons, in a wide range of circumstances. Yet within this morally charged atmosphere there is a real danger that the public will view the involvement of the state in a person's family life as confirmation that they must therefore be a threat to law and order.

On a similar theme, le Grand's article (Chapter Three) suggests that through our profession's identification with the state we could be contributing to the continuation of some negative stereotypes by simply doing our jobs. Le Grand writes that the 'chav' persona – as it has come to be constructed by the media – is defined by their unwillingness to financially support themselves (or their dependents), and their wish to rely on social welfare agencies. So by being the profession that works closest with those poor, white, working-class young men and women and their families who are labelled as 'chavs', we are – in the public's mind – confirming the caricature. But as social workers, we are accustomed to working alongside those people who are misunderstood, and often maligned by the media or powerful sections of society: we are adept at uncovering the complex human stories that exist behind the malicious myths. During my career, I have met the proud but harried single mother struggling to get by on 'too generous' state benefits who, in desperation, resorts to a pay-day loan company; I have listened to the man who explained that after being released from prison he lived in homeless accommodation for two years and, overwhelmed by a sense of hopelessness, returned to using heroin; I too was told to 'f*** off' by the young person hanging around the shopping centre during the school day, hood closed tightly over her face, projecting an image of menace to hide her vulnerability.

As somebody who has worked in local government for over 10 years, I see a virtue in public service; I am enormously proud of the positive difference the state has made, and continues to make, to millions of people's lives through the National Health Service, the education system, plus targeted services like statutory social work. It was therefore troubling to read how the state's reaction to a moral panic can actually create further harm for individuals. In Chapter One Greer highlights that, in response to public fears about seemingly irresponsible teenagers accessing inappropriate material on the internet, the government endorsed the increased use of filters to block certain content. However, this move meant that some young people became unable to visit websites that provided valuable information about suicide, safe sex or LGBT identity issues. As moral panics often scapegoat one particular social, cultural or ethnic group in society, seeking to portray them as the source of a perceived crisis, how the state decides to respond in such high-profile situations can significantly affect the quality of relationships between different communities. One could argue that the reactions of certain politicians to Lee Rigby's murder, as discussed by McKendrick in Chapter Two, were intentionally provocative, and that they aggravated, rather than allayed, wider public distrust of those individuals who subscribe to the Islamic faith.

Yet in my mind there appears to be an important distinction between suggesting that the state deliberately uses moral panics to restrict the freedom of individuals and to generate social discord – as is perhaps suggested by Hall – as opposed to viewing these responses as lapses in good governance, sometimes leading to unintended consequences. It would seem to me that there are many instances highlighted in this book where state officials have responded to media pressure or a perceived change in public mood, arguably in a rash or ill-considered manner, but with no more sinister a motive than wanting to sway the electorate in the desired direction. But one's opinion on such issues may well depend on whether one regards the state's influence within society as something to be supported or to be viewed with suspicion: is the state our benevolent parent, trying to act with positive intentions to promote our collective best interest, or is it a nefarious tyrant, naturally prone toward negative forms of social control? In reality it is probably neither fully the one nor the other; encompassing many diverse and competing institutions, interests and ideas, the modern state seems both biased towards preserving existing power structures while also trying to protect some semblance of a humane and civilised society within a ruthless, global capitalist system (with arguably limited success).

In order for the state to respond more effectively to moral panics, we must begin with an acknowledgement that many ordinary people will (and are entitled to) feel unease with various types of social change;

and, left unaddressed, such anxieties can morph into something more sinister. Parton (2005) has written about the controversial 'name and shame' campaign undertaken by the *News of the World* newspaper in 2000 following Sarah Payne's murder by a predatory sex offender, and how this triggered a wave of vigilante-style attacks on the suspected homes of alleged paedophiles. Though it was apparent that the actions of the media were fuelling public alarm and influencing the political agenda – and thus a moral panic was seemingly in progress – Parton also argues that we should not lose sight of the fact that those parents living with their families in the predominantly working-class communities where the state had chosen to resettle a number of convicted sex offenders, without any prior public consultation, were likely to feel shocked and scared. It is a depressing fact that headlines that play on parents' fears about their children's safety are likely to sell more newspapers. However, in these circumstances the media did not conjure up a moral panic 'out of nothing', so to speak; they responded, perhaps irresponsibly, to pre-existing concerns.

It is no longer good enough to dismiss moral panics as being the irrational over-reaction of a naïve public, duped by unscrupulous media moguls or power-hungry politicians. This stance runs the risk of denying ordinary people a voice. Drawing on the lessons of the Left Realist school of criminology, pioneered by Kinsey et al (1986), we should accept the public's fears as legitimate and meet them head on. It is vital that the state should begin to listen, learn and lead a response to people's views on the many difficult and divisive social issues that characterise modern society. I would see social work as being at the forefront of this bold and proactive strategy: dispensing with the moral rhetoric and political posturing that dominate much public discussion, practitioners can engage people in honest, straightforward conversations on subjects such as who actually commits sexual offences and what really works in reducing re-offending; what was the full range of social and economic factors that contributed to civil disobedience in London during the summer of 2011; what are the different social costs and benefits associated with new technologies such as the internet.

I was intrigued by Kirkwood's (Chapter Four) thoughts on the discursive dimension to a moral panic and the enormous power that resides in language to shape social realities. An official, state-approved discourse pervades press releases, policy documentation, the speeches of politicians in Parliament, and tells it 'like it is' to the public – what the problems are that we face, who is to blame and what should be done about them. Social work practitioners, armed with a knowledge of moral panic theory, especially the work of Hall, can start to decipher and disrupt this dominant discourse. Just as there is the potential within language to shape social reality in a negative way – to denigrate white, working-class youths as 'chavs', to depict vulnerable families as a threat to law and order, to deny young people the autonomy to enjoy modern technology – as social workers we can offer a different perspective: one informed by a progressive set of values based on notions of respect, tolerance and fairness. Through this discourse we can positively shape society – dismantling the myths and stereotypes that poison public attitudes and robustly proclaiming the advantages of social cohesion.

References

Hall, S., Critcher, C., Jefferson, T., Clarke, J. and Roberts, B. (1978) *Policing the crisis: Mugging, the state, and law and order*, London: Macmillan.

Kinsey, R., Lea., J. and Young, J. (1986) *Losing the fight against crime*, London: Blackwell.

Parton, N. (2005) *Safeguarding childhood: Early intervention and surveillance in late modern society*, London: Palgrave Macmillan.

Weber, M. (1994 [1919]) 'The profession and vocation of politics', in P. Lassman and R. Speirs (eds) *Weber: Political writings*, Cambridge: Cambridge University Press.